THE KINGFISHER
GUIDE TO
CONSERVATORY
PLANTS

Key to coloured tabs

The plants in this book are divided into the groups listed below. Use the coloured tab in the corner of the pages to help you find the different groups as you flick through the book. Within each group the plants are arranged alphabetically.

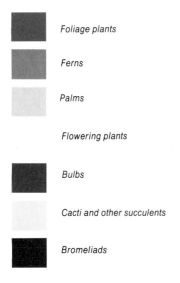

Foliage plants

Ferns

Palms

Flowering plants

Bulbs

Cacti and other succulents

Bromeliads

THE KINGFISHER

GUIDE TO

CONSERVATORY

❧ PLANTS ❧

KEN MARCH • JILL THOMAS

Kingfisher Books

Kingfisher Books, Grisewood & Dempsey Ltd
Elsley House, 24–30 Great Titchfield Street,
London W1P 7AD

First published in 1993 by Kingfisher Books

10 9 8 7 6 5 4 3 2 1

Some of the material in this book was
previously published by Kingfisher Books in
Kingfisher Guide to Indoor Plants in 1991 and
*Kingfisher Complete Guide to Indoor &
Conservatory Plants* in 1992.

BRITISH LIBRARY CATALOGUING IN PUBLICATION DATA
A catalogue record for this book is available
from the British Library.

ISBN 1 85697 043 4

Editor: Stuart Cooper
Consultant: Brian Davis
Artwork: Jonathan Adams, Wendy Bramall,
John Davis, Will Giles, Sandra Pond

Printed in Portugal

CONTENTS

INTRODUCTION

The benefits provided by a conservatory are tremendous. Properly planned, constructed and maintained, it is an ideal location in which to cultivate numerous plant varieties that cannot be grown successfully either in the garden or indoors. It is a special place that enables the gardener to enjoy the pleasures of gardening all year round, as well as a retreat in which to relax and reflect with only beautiful plants and ornaments for company.

The wide variety of plants available for the conservatory means there is something to suit almost every taste, growing environment and level of horticultural skill. Elegant palms can be used to give a feeling of days gone by, while bold plants, such as *Strelitzia reginae*, produce striking effects. Damp, shady conservatories can be filled with ferns; warm, dry conservatories are ideal for growing cacti and other succulents. Novice gardeners can achieve success with hardy ivies, then move on to the more demanding exotics, such as bromeliads.

The enjoyment of plants in the conservatory is enhanced by the many different techniques that have been developed for displaying them. Container manufacturers produce a vast array of pots, wall pots, hanging pots and baskets, planters and troughs in which to grow plants. Conservatories also offer the opportunity to create open soil beds, in which many varieties can be grown almost to their full natural size.

The key to growing plants successfully lies in understanding and responding to their needs. They must be provided with just the right amount of warmth, light, humidity, water and food; potted in the correct pot containing a suitable compost; and placed in the best position. This book gives detailed instructions on all these points for over 200 of the most attractive, interesting and unusual varieties that are suitable for growing in the conservatory.

Plant names
Most conservatory plants have a common name, e.g. Black-eyed Susan, and they all have a botanical name, e.g. *Thunbergia alata*. While the common name may be easier to remember, the botanical name should be used to identify and order plants. Apart from the fact that all plants have a botanical name, this name is also unique to each plant. Botanical names are also internationally recognized and more stable, although they do change from time to time as our understanding of plant relationships advances. This book gives any former or alternative botanical names.

Botanical names usually have two components, denoting the genus (*Thunbergia*) and the species (*alata*). Some names also have a third component. If this begins with a lower-case letter the plant is a subspecies; if it starts with a capital letter and is in quotation marks the plant is a hybrid that has been raised in cultivation. Because of limitations of space, it has not always been possible to list all the hybrids or subspecies of each plant in this book.

Introduction

HOW TO USE THIS BOOK

The plants in this book are presented as single-page entries that focus on a single species, on a species and its varieties, or on a group of closely related plants. Each entry contains a concise description of the plant or plants, including any common or alternative botanical names that are used; a photograph for identification; a facts panel that lists the plant's physical characteristics, season of interest, care requirements, availability, uses and the related varieties; and a line drawing that illustrates a useful care, display or propagation method. All these features are identified and described in the panel below. For those unfamiliar with them, the terms used to describe plant characteristics are explained on page 9 of the Introduction.

There are a number of ways in which this book can be used to select plants for the conservatory. Refer to the index to find a particular plant, the colour key to flick through a specific group of plants, the photographs to work out schemes for associated planting, and the facts panel for selecting the varieties that might suit or grow well in a particular type of conservatory or location within one.

This colour shows which group of plants each variety belongs to. The colour codes are explained on the second page of the book.

This is the current botanical name for the plant. Use it to identify, order and select plants.

A colour photograph shows each plant against a plain background, which allows the main features to stand out.

A text summarizes the main features of the plant and elaborates on the care, display or propagation methods. It also gives any alternative botanical names.

The common name or names may help to verify the identity of a plant but common names are not universal so do not use them when ordering plants.

A facts panel provides all the information needed to cultivate, display and propagate each plant, together with physical characters for identification and details of related varieties.

A line drawing shows how to perform an operation relating to care or propagation, or illustrates one of the display suggestions.

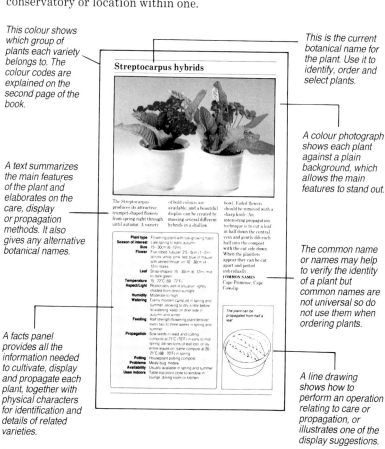

Streptocarpus hybrids

The Streptocarpus produces its attractive trumpet-shaped flowers from spring right through until autumn. A variety of bold colours are available, and a beautiful display can be created by massing several different hybrids in a shallow bowl. Faded flowers should be removed with a sharp knife. An interesting propagation technique is to cut a leaf in half down the central vein and gently dib each half into the compost with the cut side down. When the plantlets appear they can be cut apart and potted individually.

COMMON NAMES Cape Primrose, Cape Cowslip

Plant type	Flowering plant with low-growing habit
Season of interest	Late spring to early autumn
Size	15 - 30cm (6 - 12in)
Flower	Five-lobed tubular 2.5 - 5cm (1 - 2in) across, white, pink, red, blue or mauve with veined throat on 10 - 30cm (4 - 12in) stalks
Leaf	Strap-shaped, 15 - 30cm (6 - 12in) mid-to dark green
Temperature	15 - 22°C (59 - 72°F)
Aspect/Light	Reasonably well-lit situation, lightly shaded from direct sunlight
Humidity	Moderate to high
Watering	Evenly moisten compost in spring and summer, allowing to dry a little before re-watering; keep on drier side in autumn and winter
Feeding	Half strength flowering plant fertiliser every two to three weeks in spring and summer
Propagation	Sow seeds in seed and cutting compost at 21°C (70°F) in early to mid spring; dib sections of leaf into, or lay entire leaves on, same compost at 20 - 21°C (68 - 70°F) in spring
Potting	Houseplant potting compost
Problems	Mealy bug, mildew
Availability	Usually available in spring and summer
Uses indoors	Table-top plant close to window in lounge, dining room or kitchen

The plant can be propagated from half a leaf

Introduction

PLANT TYPES AND CHARACTERISTICS

The following sections outline the groups into which the plants in this book are divided, and explain the terms used to describe plant characteristics. These groupings are a mixture of traditional and scientific categories and are the ones most used in retail outlets and suppliers' catalogues.

Foliage plants
All foliage plants produce flowers but they are usually insignificant. These plants are grown mainly for their leaves, which may be green or variegated, or more unusual colours such as yellow and red. The leaves of some plants change colour in the autumn. Leaves may be hand-shaped, oval, lance-shaped or divided into leaflets. Many are toothed.

Ferns
Ferns bear no flowers but reproduce by dispersing spores. These are borne on the underside of leaves, known as fronds, which are either bold and tongue-shaped or divided into leaflets.

Palms
Palms produce flowers but their main attraction lies in the arching, finely divided leaves, which are known as fronds, as in the ferns. Palms are slow-growing plants and are relatively easy to maintain.

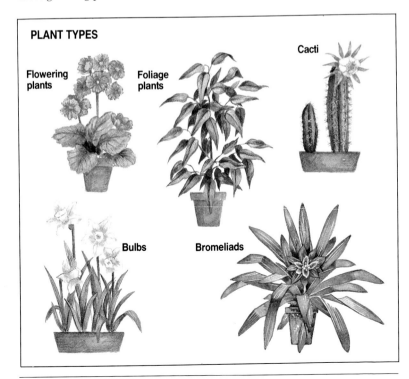

PLANT TYPES

Flowering plants

Foliage plants

Cacti

Bulbs

Bromeliads

Introduction

Flowering plants
Flowering plants are grown mainly for their flowers although some also produce berries and fruits. Plants come into flower in all seasons of the year and some produce blooms all year round. The duration of flowering varies with each plant, ranging from just a few days to several months.

Bulbs
Bulbs are also flowering plants but they are usually put in a separate group because of their growing needs. The bulb is the plant's storage organ. True bulbs consist of fleshy scales surrounding a central bud, but the term is also used for other storage organs such as corms and tubers.

Cacti and other succulents
Cacti do not bear leaves but have instead thick, succulent stems, which store water. Many varieties are spiny or hairy. Other succulents have thick, fleshy stems and leaves, which also act as water reservoirs.

Bromeliads
Bromeliads produce a rosette of glossy green foliage and a vividly coloured flower head or spike. The spike is formed by a series of modified leaves called bracts; the flowers themselves are small and insignificant.

Habit
Each of the plant type descriptions in the facts panels also include details of the plant's habit. This is the overall shape and direction of the growth and may be erect, upright, bushy, shrubby, prostrate, trailing or climbing.

Season of interest
This is the period during which a plant is considered to be at its most attractive. For the foliage plants, ferns, palms, bromeliads and many of the cacti, this tends to be all year round. For the flowering plants, bulbs and some cacti it is generally the flowering period.

Size
The sizes given in this book are the ranges within which the plants are considered to look at their best and are practical to keep. Plants grown in conservatory beds can reach the upper end of this range. Container-grown plants are constrained in size both by the limited space for root development and the need to keep them to a manageable size by pruning.

Flower
In the flowering plants, bulbs, cacti and bromeliads the flowers or flower heads are a major feature of the plant and are covered in some detail. In the groups where flowers are insignificant they are described only briefly.

Leaf
The leaves are described to aid selection and to facilitate the identification of unknown plants. The descriptions are for plants that are in good health; the foliage of unhealthy plants may appear quite different.

Introduction

PLANT CARE AND CULTIVATION

This book provides specific instructions on care and cultivation for every plant included. The following sections give some general advice on each aspect of plant care.

Temperature
The temperature range given for each plant is the optimum at which it will sustain its rate of growth and overall health. It is essential to provide a stable temperature, preferably towards the middle of the range. Plants that are kept too warm during the day and then too cold at night often shed their foliage. For the same reason it is important to keep plants away from draughts.

Problems caused by temperature occur most often in late autumn, winter and early spring, when many plants are in their vulnerable resting phase and fluctuations of heat and cold are most likely.

Aspect/Light
All plants need light to manufacture the foods that enable them to grow and produce healthy foliage and flowers. The amount of light needed varies between the different species so the positioning of plants is of vital importance. Ferns prefer rather more shade than other plants as their deep green foliage has evolved to collect relatively low levels of light. Conversely, highly coloured foliage plants will lose their bright colours if they are deprived of the sunlight that creates them.

Humidity
The amount of atmospheric moisture a plant needs depends upon the rate the water drawn up from its roots is lost through its leaves – the process known as transpiration. Cacti and other succulents have fleshy tissue, which can store water, so they do not need high humidity. Ferns and some other plants have thin leaves, which lose water rapidly. If the air is too dry they will soon become shrivelled and turn brown at the leaf edges.

Most problems occur with plants that require high humidity, as many conservatories have a dry atmosphere. Misting helps to increase humidity but with species that also need bright sun, this can cause marking of the foliage. Another solution is to place the pot on moist pebbles so that moisture evaporates below the plant. Another technique is to group plants in a bowl or planter so they create a humid microclimate. A water feature, such as an indoor pool, will also help to raise the humidity level.

Watering
More plants fail because of problems with watering than for any other reason. The amount of water needed varies greatly between the different groups of plants, and it is also dependent on temperature, light, time of year, size of pot, and even air movement.

Tap water is acceptable for most plants, although it should be allowed to adjust to room temperature before use. If rainwater is recommended, the rain should be collected and stored hygienically.

A bed of pebbles, half covered with water, will help to maintain humidity.

Humidity can also be provided by regularly misting the foliage with tepid water.

Most plants can safely be provided with water through the surface of the compost, as long as it is allowed to drain into a saucer below and the surplus is discarded. Unless the plant is an aquatic species it should not be left standing in water, otherwise the roots will rot.

If your budget allows there are a number of very effective watering devices that eliminate the need for manual watering, such as automatic drip systems and capillary matting irrigation systems.

Frequency of watering is also important. Ferns and some other plants should be kept constantly moist. Cacti and succulents should be watered infrequently, with more in the spring and summer when they are actively growing, but the barest minimum in autumn and winter. With most other plants it is usually a good policy to allow the compost to get on the dry side before re-watering. Do not let it dry out too much as the plant will wilt and the compost will shrink back from the pot and allow water to drain away rather than absorbing it.

Not all plants that wilt are too dry; they often wilt when they are too wet. It is therefore important to judge the condition of the compost very carefully before watering by probing beneath the surface with a finger.

Feeding

Feeding should take place only during a plant's active growing season. Moisten the compost before applying the fertilizer and ensure that it is used at the strength recommended for the plant.

The type of fertilizer to use depends on the plant and its stage of growth. A general houseplant fertilizer, high in nitrogen, can be used for most foliage and flowering plants to promote lush foliage. With flowering plants, once the foliage is established it is best to switch to a flowering plant fertilizer, rich in potassium. This will produce better flowers.

Slow-release fertilizers save the trouble of mixing and can be applied as pellets or sticks that are sprinkled over, or inserted into, the compost.

Introduction

Training

Plants with a climbing habit of growth need some means of support. Small, pot-grown plants, such as *Philodendron scandens*, simply require a small stick or stake, while loose, leggy plants should be provided with a light framework of sticks placed around the pot and linked together with string. Climbing plants with a bushy habit need a trellis or hoop. In all these cases, carefully attach the plant to the support with small wire split rings or soft string.

More vigorous plants need a moss pole for support. Attach the plant to the pole with string, hairpins or pegs formed from bent wire, and moisten the pole regularly with a mister. Some plants that both climb and trail, such as *Hedera canariensis variegata*, can be grown in a hanging pot or basket in which the stems will both hang over the sides and climb up the supporting ropes or chains.

Large-growing climbing plants, such as *Jasminum polyanthum*, can be trained up the walls of the conservatory. The stems should be tied to galvanized or plastic-coated wires, which are attached to the wall with eyed screws called vine eyes. The wires should be placed at intervals of about 18in (50cm) up the wall, and no more than 10ft (3m) should be allowed between the vine eyes in any straight line. Plants that have a more rigid growth pattern, such as peaches, can be trained up canes tied to the wire support in a fan-shape. With the Clematis, vertical wires tied to the horizontal wires every 30cm (12in) will make an open net that is ideal for the leaf tendrils to cling to.

Several plants that are grown in the conservatory can be trained up the walls and along the ridge of the roof, again using wire and vine eyes for support. This method of training is of particular benefit to those plants that need exposure to direct sunlight, such as *Hoya carnosa*. It is also a means of providing an area of shade in which to grown plants that require less light.

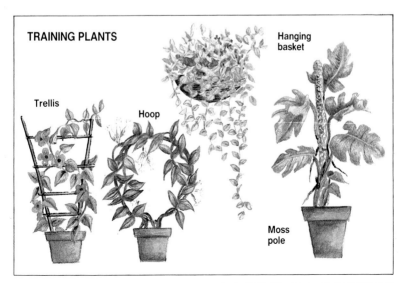

TRAINING PLANTS

Hanging basket

Trellis

Hoop

Moss pole

When roots fill the pot, knock out the plant, keeping the root ball intact.

Place the old pot into a slightly larger one and fill around with compost.

Remove the old pot, place the root ball in the hole, firm around the sides, and water.

Potting

Repotting into a larger pot is necessary not only to provide a plant with more space for its roots but also to increase the reserve of nutrients and the moisture-retaining capacity, and to give the plant more stability. Repotting is best carried out in the plant's growing season. Frequency depends on the plant, but once every two to three years is enough for most varieties. Select a pot that is no more than 7.5–10cm (3–4in) larger in diameter than the previous one. Do not re-pot plants that are diseased or stressed. When plants reach a certain size it may be impractical to re-pot them into a larger pot so replace the compost in the existing pot every three years or so.

All the plants in this book can be grown in ordinary houseplant potting compost. However, when potting cacti and succulents, orchids or bromeliads, try to obtain the composts that are produced for these plants.

Conservatory beds

Conservatory beds provide additional space for root development and are therefore ideal for growing many of the larger varieties. They also enable the conservatory gardener to create highly attractive mixed plantings.

Beds are either made at ground level by opening up an area in the conservatory floor, built with brick walls, or both let into the floor and built up, for extra soil depth. Whatever type of bed is preferred, it must be a minimum of 50cm (18in) deep, and 80–100cm (31–40in) wide.

Good drainage is essential so put a 10–15cm (4–6in) layer of drainage material, such as rubble, in the bottom of the bed. Fill the bed up with a high-quality soil-based potting compost. If there is no soil access to the conservatory bed it will be necessary to use a layer of drainage material that is at least 30cm (12in) deep and to lay a pipe that will carry water away from the conservatory to a soakaway.

Introduction

Pruning
Pruning is necessary to maintain a compact habit and to encourage bushy growth. In most cases it is simply a matter of pinching out the foliage using the thumb and forefinger. Woody-stemmed subjects, however, require the use of secateurs or a pruning knife, and plants with very thick stems must be pruned with a saw.

It is important when pruning to leave a clean wound with no bruised or ragged tissue that could become infected with disease. Trim back to a position just above a leaf or bud, as long lengths of bare stem can 'die back', leading to disfigurement or loss of the plant. A few species ooze a milky sap when pruned. This can be dealt with by sprinkling charcoal over the cut to congeal the sap and seal the wound.

Some plants produce leggy and untidy growth that requires rather more than a light trim. They should be cut back by a half to two thirds in the spring to produce a reasonably compact plant the following season.

Grooming and cleaning
Dead flowers and brown leaves should be pinched out or trimmed off immediately to maintain the appearance of the plant and to prevent the spread of disease. After removing diseased tissue, clean and disinfect any cutting tools before using them on other plants.

It is not usually necessary to clean leaves more than a couple of times a year. Avoid leaf shines or oily sprays as these may damage the plant. Plants with tough, waxy leaves should be wiped gently with a damp cloth to remove dust and grime. Clean the top surface only. Other plants can be cleaned by spraying the foliage with tepid water. Soak up excess water with a kitchen towel and allow the plant to dry away from sunlight.

Cleaning is best carried out when plants are actively growing; during their dormant period they are more susceptible to damage.

Pests and diseases
This section explains how to combat the pests and diseases that affect plants. Remember, though, that prevention is better than cure. A plant that has been well cared for should be strong and healthy enough to resist most infections so follow the care instructions strictly. Carry out regular check-ups for pests and diseases and put sickly plants into quarantine to prevent the problem spreading to healthy plants.

Most pests and diseases can be dealt with using the range of products detailed in the chart opposite. Follow the manufacturer's guidelines for the safe use, storage and disposal of these products. Chemicals are available in liquid concentrate or powder form to be mixed with water and applied through a mister, or as dust or aerosol sprays. Check that sprays do not contain CFCs (chlorinated fluorocarbons), which may damage the ozone layer. If possible, use sprays outdoors, but away from direct sunlight to avoid scorching the leaves. Some chemicals can be applied with a paintbrush or a cotton swab. If in doubt as to whether a chemical can be used on a plant, test it on just one or two leaves first. The use of known pest predators provides an effective and environmentally friendly form of pest control.

Aphid
Attacks soft, fleshy plants, such as flowering plants, depositing sticky honeydew and causing weak, deformed growth. Spray repeatedly with soft soap or pyrethrum.

Mealy bug
Attacks many plants, especially cacti and other succulents. Deposits honeydew and white wool, and causes deformation. Spray repeatedly with derris or apply methylated spirits to bugs with brush.

Red spider mite
Pest of many plants growing in hot, dry conditions. Causes mottling, cupping and browning of foliage; white webbing visible in severe attacks. Spray repeatedly with derris.

Mildew
Disease of relatively few plants, e.g. Begonias, Hydrangeas, Saintpaulias, leaving white powder or down and causing stunted growth. Hard to treat so dust plants with sulphur as preventative.

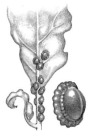

Scale insect
Affects many plants, causing deformation and leaf drop; badly affected plants turn yellow and cannot be cured. Spray young insects with pyrethrum or derris; remove adults with fingernail.

Rust
Affects few plants, e.g. Fuchsias, forming orange, brown or straw-coloured patches and damaging leaves. Hard to control, although removal of infected leaves helps.

Thrips
Attacks flowering plants, e.g. Fuchsias, Calceolarias and Cyclamens, causing flecking and distortion of flower petals, and stunted growth. Spray repeatedly with pyrethrum or derris.

Botrytis
Affects soft-fleshed plants. Fluffy grey mould forms on dead leaves or flowers then attacks live tissue. Remove dead matter before rot sets in; dust plants with sulphur as preventative.

Whitefly
Minor pest of many plants. Deposits honeydew and causes yellowing and loss of leaves. Larvae cannot be eradicated easily. Spray adult flies repeatedly with pyrethrum.

Sooty mould
Disease of plants affected by insect pests that secrete honeydew, on which sooty mould grows. Causes leaf damage and loss. Remove with mild, warm solution of detergent or soft soap.

Introduction

PROPAGATION

An enjoyable and inexpensive way of obtaining new plants is to propagate them yourself. The basic techniques of propagation are sowing and germination of seeds or spores; rooting of cuttings; layering; and separation and rooting of offsets. The text entries describe the method or methods to use for each plant and the following sections provide some general guidelines on each technique. Follow the instructions carefully and make sure that pots, trays, knives, scissors and other tools are spotlessly clean, preferably sterile. Use only proprietary potting composts, never garden soil as it may contain harmful disease organisms. The best time to propagate plants is early in their growing season, which for most varieties is spring or summer. At that time, not only will conditions will be right for germination or rooting, but the young plant will have sufficient time to grow on and become established in readiness for the traumas of winter.

Seeds or fern spores

Fill a seed tray or half pot with seed sowing compost and sprinkle the seeds or spores thinly on the surface. If the seeds are small to large, cover them lightly with compost. Very fine seeds or spores should be left uncovered. Moisten the compost with a fine-rosed watering can or a mister. Cover the container with glass and maintain the temperature at 19–24°C (66–75°F). Once the seeds or spores have germinated, remove the cover; do not leave the seedlings under cover or the growth will become soft and leggy. Prick out the seedlings when they are large enough to handle and pot them singly.

Cuttings

There are several methods for propagating plants from cuttings, using either the growing tips and stems, the stems by themselves, or the leaves. Cuttings should be taken only from plants that are healthy.

To take a tip cutting, cut off the growing tip and a 5–10cm (2–4in) section of stem using a sharp knife; for a stem cutting, remove a similar length of stem. Dip the stem into hormone rooting powder and insert the cuttings into a pot of seed and cutting compost. Cover the pot with a polythene bag supported on a stick frame and keep the compost moist. Keep the temperature at 19–24°C (66–75°F). Some plants can be propagated by laying sections of stem on the surface of the compost. Keep it moist and maintain the temperature within the range given above.

A tip cutting consists of the growing tip and a short piece of stem. Dip the base of the stem in rooting powder and insert it half way into the compost. Cover with a polythene bag.

Leaf cuttings provide a simple and fascinating method for obtaining several varieties. *Begonia masoniana* can be propagated by pegging a whole leaf, upperside down, on to the compost and cutting incisions in the main veins. Streptocarpus can be propagated by cutting a leaf in half along its length and inserting the two cut sides into the compost. All these methods lead to the production of tiny plantlets, which can be removed and potted when they are large enough to handle.

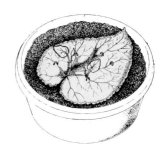

To propagate Begonia rex, *peg a whole leaf, with the veins cut, onto the compost. Alternatively, cut a leaf into postage-stamp sized sections and lay them on the compost.*

Offsets and rhizomes

Some plants, such as *Strelitzia reginae*, form miniature plants as side shoots from the main stem. These 'offsets' can be teased away and potted. Moisten the compost first to make separation easier. When propagating cacti from offsets, wear protective gloves and do not over-moisten the compost. Treat bromeliads gently as the offsets are easily damaged.

Several plants grow in clumps or rosettes, which can be separated and planted. Remove some compost to expose the thick stem or rhizome which connects the clump to the rest of the plant and break the join by hand or with a sharp knife. Do not just cut the plant in two.

Layering

Layering is the technique used to propagate some trailing plants, such as the Chlorophytum, which produce plantlets on the stems or leaves. Allow the plantlets to rest in a pot filled with seed and cutting compost and they will readily root. Some plants, such as Ficus species, can be forced to produce plantlets from sections of stem, a process known as air layering. Cut half way into the centre of the stem and then up about 5cm (2in). Partially open the wound, dust it with rooting powder, and pack moist sphagnum moss between and around the cut. Wrap polythene around the moss and wait several weeks until roots form and fill the area. The plantlet can then be removed and potted.

The Chlorophytum *produces plantlets on the ends of its long stems. These can be pegged into separate pots and when they take root and start growing the stems can be cut.*

Introduction

CONSERVATORIES

The practicalities of constructing a conservatory are beyond the scope of this book but it is possible to give some general guidelines on planning or choosing a conservatory and on displaying plants within it.

Conservatory types
Conservatories come in a wide range of styles, shapes, sizes and materials. Cost is important when deciding on a conservatory but remember that it is to be part of your home and you will expect it to last for many years. Always ensure that your choice enhances the value of your property and that the style you choose is sympathetic to the existing building. Furthermore, ensure that the conservatory is made of materials that are suitable for the purpose and that maintenance will be kept to a minimum. It is advisable when considering these points to seek the advice of a specialist supplier or consultant.

Styles of conservatory vary from the modern, with its square, clean-cut lines, to the more ornate Victorian-type building. Today most conservatories are of the lean-to type and are connected to the house as an additional room. However, other types are available that can be situated away from the house, against a suitable garden wall. Free-standing conservatories, which can be sited in any suitable area within the garden, provide yet another option.

With larger conservatories it may be possible to divide the internal area into closed-off sections in which to create different growing environments and thereby increase the range of plants grown.

Whatever type of conservatory you choose or have built, ensure that the doors and windows can be locked securely.

Conservatory essentials
It is vital at the outset to decide if the conservatory is to be used mainly for growing plants or if it is to form another living room for people in which plants merely provide decoration. As the needs of plants and people rarely coincide, this decision will have a bearing on the range of plants that are grown and therefore on the conditions that will have to be created to provide them with the proper care.

When constructing the conservatory, make sure you adhere to any planning and building regulations. The conservatory should have a tap and some means of heating for winter. Have electricity installed by an approved electrician and ensure it is insulated from damp. Lay rot-proof flooring, such as tiles, so you can douse it with water to create humidity.

Heating
Electric heaters, particularly those with a thermostat to control the heat level, and those with fans that circulate the air, are the most efficient way of heating the conservatory.

Gas heaters – fuelled by either natural gas or propane – can be used, as can oil heaters. However, more care and management is needed with both types of heating.

It may be possible to connect the central heating system of the house to the conservatory. However, in most systems the house heating is turned off at night, just when plants require it most, so a bypass may be needed.

To save on fuel bills, it is worth dividing the conservatory into two in winter so that you can put the plants that require heat into one half and heat that half only.

Ventilation

The conservatory should be properly ventilated to prevent the atmosphere becoming too dry and to reduce problems with pests and diseases. Ventilation should even be provided in winter.

The most effective way of managing the air flow is to have air vents at ground level, in the walls and in the roof. If your budget allows, a system can be purchased which controls the vents automatically.

In addition to vents, electric roof fans can be used to keep the air cool. Again, electronically controlled fans are available.

If, during spring or summer, you want to leave the conservatory door or windows open to increase ventilation, it might be necessary to use a wire screen to keep out cats, birds and insect pests.

Shading

Most conservatories will need some form of shading to avoid exposing the plants to hot summer sun, and as another method of temperature control.

Special paints are available which reduce the intensity of sunlight, and they can be removed from the glass in winter.

Shade netting is useful, and can be fitted permanently or temporarily. Like internal or external roller blinds, netting can be automatically controlled as the weather dictates.

Furnishings and ornaments

If the conservatory is to be used primarily for growing plants, furniture should be kept to a minimum. Any furniture that is used should be moisture-resistant as the atmosphere must be kept damp for the plants.

If space permits, statuary and other ornaments can greatly enhance a conservatory. Ornaments that are sold specifically for conservatory or garden use are best as they should be moisture-resistant.

Using plants in the conservatory

Most plants that can be grown indoors are also suitable for the conservatory. However, if you wish to use your conservatory mainly for growing plants it would be a shame not to take advantage of the opportunities that the space and the controlled environment of the conservatory offers. Many of the larger, more exotic plants – which cannot be grown either indoors or in the garden – are ideal for the conservatory. They can be displayed in many different ways – trained up trellises or walls, trailed from statues, grown in ornamental troughs or urns, planted around an indoor pool, or grown in conservatory beds. A wide range of associated plantings – including seasonal displays – can be created using plants of every kind, shape and size.

Araucaria heterophylla

The Araucaria is a superb plant for the enthusiast who likes a plant of regular geometrical shape. However, the radiating growth will only be achieved by providing the plant with even light and sufficient space to grow and develop. Failure to do so will result in growth that is somewhat lopsided, which almost ruins the effect of the plant. This species is closely related to the Monkey Puzzle Tree, which grows in gardens, but it is not hardy outside. However, it does share some similar characteristics in that the needles become sharp as they mature. As the plant becomes older the needles tend to drop off, as do the branches, creating a mess on the floor. The plant is best cleaned by using a pressure water mister to wash the dust off, thus allowing the natural sheen to show through.

COMMON NAME
Norfolk Island Pine

Plant type	Foliage plant with radiating branches on evenly shaped erect habit
Season of interest	All year round
Size	100 – 300cm (39 – 117in)
Flower	None
Leaf	Green needles, 0.5 –1cm ($\frac{1}{4}$in – $\frac{1}{3}$in), which become harder and sharper as they mature, on branches 30 – 60cm (12 – 24in)
Temperature	10 – 20°C (50 – 68°F)
Aspect/Light	Moderate to reasonably bright, but dislikes prolonged exposure to direct sunlight
Humidity	Moderate
Watering	Evenly moisten compost in spring and summer; keep on the dry side in autumn and winter
Feeding	Once every three to four weeks with houseplant fertilizer in spring and summer
Propagation	Sow seeds in pans at 18 – 20°C (65 – 68°F) from mid spring to early summer in seed and cutting compost
Potting	Houseplant potting compost
Problems	Mealy bug, root mealy bug, premature loss of lower leaves
Availability	Occasionally available throughout year
Uses	Grow in a container at floor level, either on its own or to give height to displays; can also be brought indoors to use as Christmas tree

Spray the foliage to clean off dust

Begonia masoniana

The foliage of this Begonia is most curious, being extremely crinkled and pitted, and bearing a dark brown pattern suggestive of the Iron Cross – hence the common name. An ideal plant for grouping or for a container display, it is a little less tolerant of windowsill cultivation. Not only is it more susceptible to root rot caused by over-watering, often coupled with lower temperatures, but the green pigment can fade if it is exposed to too much light. The crinkled leaves can become dusty and should be gently rinsed with tepid water. Shake off any excess moisture and leave the plant to dry well away from sunlight.

COMMON NAME
Iron Cross Begonia

Plant type	Foliage plant with compact and somewhat horizontal growth
Season of interest	All year round
Size	10–20cm (4–8in)
Flower	Infrequent, greenish, insignificant, 0.6cm (¼in)
Leaf	Unusual, roughly heart-shaped, very crinkled with slight serration; green with dark brown 'Iron Cross' pattern, 7.5–12.5cm (3–5in)
Temperature	18–20°C (65–68°F)
Aspect/Light	Moderate light with some shade
Humidity	Average to high
Watering	Keep compost moderately moist in spring and summer; keep on dry side in autumn and winter
Feeding	Once every two weeks with half strength houseplant fertilizer in spring and summer
Propagation	5cm (2in) sections of rhizome with leaves, or leaf cuttings, at 21°C (70°F) in spring or summer in houseplant potting compost
Potting	Houseplant potting compost
Problems	Root rot, leggy growth, bleaching of leaves in too much light
Availability	Occasionally available, particularly in spring or summer
Uses	Grow in a container either on its own or as part of a group display

Remove dust from the leaves with a spray of tepid water

Chlorophytum comosum 'Vittatum'

The Chlorophytum is one of the most common and popular plants, and is quite tolerant of a variety of conditions. It can be used in mixed plantings, but due to its vigour it is probably best not planted in constrained areas as it will soon outgrow them.

With its characteristic arching and trailing stems, the Chlorophytum is particularly good as a hanging plant in a wall pot or in a basket suspended from the roof of the conservatory. To maintain the plant's appearance, trim off brown leaf tips with sharp scissors, taking care to leave a small area of dead tissue.

COMMON NAMES
St Bernard's Lily, Spider Plant

Plant type	Foliage plant with divergent habit and trailing stems producing plantlets
Season of interest	All year round
Size	20–40cm (8–16in)
Flower	Tiny, white, on ends of long trailing stems, produced in spring and summer
Leaf	Grass-like, cascading in splayed fashion, 46–61cm (18–24in), succulent, green and white striped
Temperature	10–18°C (50–65°F)
Aspect/Light	Well-lit situation, out of direct sunlight
Humidity	Moderate
Watering	Keep compost evenly moist in spring and summer; keep drier in autumn and winter
Feeding	Once every two to four weeks with houseplant fertilizer in spring and summer
Propagation	Root plantlets in houseplant potting compost or water in spring and summer at 18–20°C (65–68°F)
Potting	Houseplant potting compost
Problems	Aphid, leaf scorch with too much sun, browning of tips in dry air
Availability	Commonly available throughout year
Uses	Grow on in its own in container or in hanging pot or basket
Other varieties	C. c. 'Picturatum' – green leaves with yellow stripe C. c. 'Variegatum' – green-edged white leaves

The plant can be propagated from plantlets produced on the trailing stems

Coleus blumei

This Coleus is one of the most popular and common of indoor plants. It is suitable for using in almost any location where there is direct sunlight to brighten the colour pigments in the leaves. The plant is also a very easy species to grow and can be shaped very simply by pinching out the terminal shoots. These same shoots provide ideal propagation material when they are large enough, and can be fun to root in water, where the roots can be watched developing. The small flowers are rather disappointing and may be cut off if not wanted. After the first season of growth, the Coleus becomes rather leggy, so it is best treated as an annual to be discarded and renewed each year. Propagate new plants from the terminal shoots.

COMMON NAMES
Flame Nettle, Painted Nettle

Pinching out the terminal shoots helps to improve bushiness

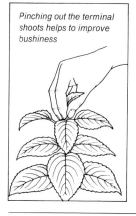

Plant type	Foliage plant with bushy habit
Season of interest	All year round
Size	30–60cm (12–24in)
Flower	Insignificant, blue, amongst foliage, produced in late spring/summer
Leaf	Pointed, oval, 5–7.5cm (2–3in), with variable coloration and bold patterning, ranging from white to pink, orange, red and green
Temperature	15–18°C (60–65°F)
Aspect/Light	Full light, some direct sunlight
Humidity	Reasonable, but requires more humidity as temperature increases
Watering	Evenly moisten compost throughout year
Feeding	Houseplant fertilizer once every two weeks in spring and summer
Propagation	Plant tip cuttings, 5–7.5cm (2–3in), from mid summer to autumn in seed and cutting compost or in water at 18–20°C (65–68°F)
Potting	Houseplant potting compost
Problems	Red spider mite, legginess as plant gets older
Availability	Commonly available in spring and early summer
Uses	Grow in container; useful for mixed plantings

Cycas revoluta

Although it has the common name of Sago Palm, the Cycas is not a species of palm at all and is only palm-like in appearance. It is one of the most primitive plants, dating back many millions of years. It is thought to be the food plant of dinosaurs, and the toughness of the leaves might be one reason why the dinosaur became extinct! The Cycas is extremely slow-growing, putting out just one new leaf each year. Eventually it forms an attractive rosette of arching plumes. Because of its lack of vigour and slow root action and development, this plant is very susceptible to over-watering, which causes the leaves to turn yellow. These should be removed with a sharp knife.

COMMON NAME
Sago Palm

Plant type	Foliage plant with radiating plumes of semi-erect foliage
Season of interest	All year round
Size	30–90cm (12–36in)
Flower	None as houseplant
Leaf	Tough leaflets, 5–15cm (2–6in) long, green, borne on stems 15–90cm (6–36in) long, forming feather-like appearance, radiating from central cone
Temperature	15–21°C (60–70°F)
Aspect/Light	Brightly lit situation
Humidity	Moderate
Watering	Evenly moisten compost in spring and summer; keep on dry side when dormant in autumn and winter
Feeding	Once a month with houseplant fertilizer in spring and summer
Propagation	Sow seeds at 21–24°C (70–75°F) in seed and cutting compost in late spring to early summer; germination and growth very slow and uneven
Potting	Houseplant potting compost
Problems	Mealy bug, scale insect, leaf yellowing with over-watering
Availability	Occasionally available throughout year
Uses	Grow in heated conservatory; display in container either at floor level or on table top

Remove brown or damaged leaves with a sharp knife

Cyperus papyrus

Several species of Cyperus may be grown indoors but *C. papyrus* is the most suitable as a conservatory plant. This is the Papyrus from which the ancient Egyptians made paper, and is also the 'bulrush' of the bible used for making Moses' cradle. Its striking appearance – smooth green stems topped by a spectacular tuft of long, thread-like leaves – makes it a very desirable plant. It is not easy to grow as it needs warmth and plenty of moisture, and the roots must never be allowed to dry out. One of the most suitable positions for the Papyrus is beside an indoor pool, although not actually in the water.

COMMON NAME
Papyrus

Plant type	Foliage plant with upright habit
Season	All year round
Size	120–240 cm (48–96in)
Flower	Small brown tufts
Leaf	Long, thread-like, 10–25cm (4–10in) green, borne in a tuft
Temperature	16–21°C (61–70°F)
Aspect/Light	Well-lit situation, shaded from full sun
Humidity	High
Watering	Water copiously all year round and keep root ball moist at all times, but do not allow the stems to stand in water
Feeding	Every 4 weeks with houseplant fertilizer from mid spring to mid summer
Propagation	By division in spring
Potting	Peat-based potting compost
Availability	Quite commonly available throughout the year
Uses	Grow in very humid conservatory; plant in container or conservatory bed as decorative water feature

Provide the roots with moisture by standing the pot in a saucer of water

Dracaena marginata

A graceful, palm-like plant. Oddly enough, it becomes more attractive as the lower leaves are shed to produce a crown of shiny foliage atop a woody, often twisted stem. Care should be taken with the positioning of this Dracaena, as any damage to the foliage will cause the subsequent growth to be deformed for a while. If damage does occur, the plant should either be left to grow through it or cut off below the damaged area with sharp secateurs. This will encourage it to produce up to three side-shoots. Plants that become too large can be treated similarly. The sections of stem removed are suitable for propagating, but it is advisable to mark them with a felt tip pen to indicate which is the right way up.

COMMON NAMES
Silhouette Plant, Striped Dragon Tree

Plant type	Ornamental foliage plant with erect habit
Season of interest	All year round
Size	100–200cm (39–78in)
Flower	None usually as indoor plant
Leaf	Narrow, 30–45cm (12–18in) long, 1.5cm ($\frac{1}{2}$in) wide, tapering to fine point, produced in tight rosette, green
Temperature	15–21°C (59–70°F)
Aspect/Light	Slightly shady or reasonably well-lit situation
Humidity	Moderate
Watering	Barely moisten compost in spring and summer; keep on dry side in autumn and winter
Feeding	Once every two to four weeks with houseplant fertilizer in spring and summer
Propagation	Plant 10–15cm (4–6in) tip cuttings or 5–7.5cm (2–3in) stem cuttings in seed and cutting compost from late spring to summer at 24°C (75°F)
Potting	Houseplant potting compost
Problems	Mealy bug, root mealy bug, premature lower leaf loss
Availability	Commonly available throughout year
Uses	Grow in container or conservatory bed either on its own or as part of group
Other varieties	D. m. 'Tricolor' – pinkish-cream variegation; more delicate

Prune off damage to the terminal shoot

Ficus benjamina

This Ficus is a magnificent plant that provides an impressive display of gently weeping foliage. Not as hardy as many other members of the fig family, it tends to be more susceptible to root problems, normally caused by over-watering, and is very sensitive to temperature changes. Such problems inevitably result in the plant dropping its leaves, almost overnight. Draughts have a similar effect and should be avoided. The plant prefers to be grown in the body of the conservatory, where the temperature is more constant, although it likes a well-lit position. Avoid excessive sun as this will cause yellowing or scorching of the foliage. Young plants may need some support to ensure that they grow as erect as possible, although eventually they should be self-supporting. Occasional trimming can help to maintain the plant's balance.

COMMON NAME
Weeping Fig

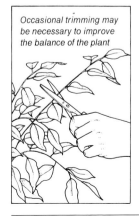

Occasional trimming may be necessary to improve the balance of the plant

Plant type	Foliage plant with erect and slightly weeping habit
Season of interest	All year round
Size	100–400cm (39–156in)
Flower	None
Leaf	Oval, pointed, 5–7.5cm (2–3in) long, 4–5cm (1½–2in) wide, green
Temperature	15–20°C (60–68°F)
Aspect/Light	Moderate to well-lit situation
Humidity	Moderate to high
Watering	Evenly moisten compost spring and summer, allowing to get on drier side before re-watering; water less in autumn and winter
Feeding	Once every two to four weeks with houseplant fertilizer from May to September
Propagation	Plant 7.5–10cm (3–4in) tip cuttings in seed and cutting compost in mid spring to early summer at 21–24°C (70–75°F)
Potting	Houseplant potting compost
Problems	Red spider mite, mealy bug, root mealy bug, scale insect; rapid leaf loss resulting from over-watering or low temperature
Availability	Commonly available throughout year
Uses	Grow in container at floor level or on low table; use on its own or in groups
Other varieties	*F. b. nuda* – thinner foliage *F. b.* 'Variegata' – variegated foliage

Ficus elastica 'Robusta'

A combination of bold foliage and great adaptability makes the Ficus an extremely popular plant. It grows as a tree in its natural habitat and can attain well over three metres (ten feet) in a large conservatory. The plant is susceptible to over-watering, which can lead to premature leaf loss and cause the remaining top leaves to droop. Cleaning and polishing of the foliage is quite a passion with some people, who seek to embellish the leaves with an artificial glossy lustre. This is quite unnecessary, and the leaves should be only gently cleaned to remove grime and dust. Occasionally, this species experiences difficulty in breaking out of dormancy, with the terminal shoot becoming hard and stunted. If this continues, remove the blind shoot to help promote the production of side shoots.

COMMON NAME
Rubber Plant

Plant type	Foliage plant with bold erect habit
Season of interest	All year round
Size	100–250cm (39–98in)
Flower	None
Leaf	15–25cm (6–10in) long, 10–15cm (4–6in) wide, oval, leathery, green
Temperature	13–20°C (55–68°F)
Aspect/Light	Medium to full light with a little shade from direct sun
Humidity	Moderate
Watering	Evenly moisten compost in spring and summer, allowing to almost dry out before re-watering; water less in autumn and winter dormancy
Feeding	Once every two to three weeks with houseplant fertilizer in spring and summer
Propagation	Plant 10–15cm (4–6in) tip cuttings, or 5–6cm (2–2½in) stem cuttings with leaf in seed and cutting compost from spring to mid summer at 27°C (80°F)
Potting	Houseplant potting compost
Problems	Aphid, red spider mite, mealy bug, scale insect, leaf loss from over-watering
Availability	Very common throughout year
Uses	Grow on its own in container or conservatory bed
Other varieties	F. e. 'Black Prince' – dark green foliage F. e. 'Decora' – more drooping leaves

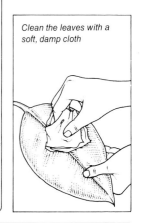

Clean the leaves with a soft, damp cloth

Ficus pumila

This Ficus is a delicate trailing and climbing plant, which looks particularly good growing up a moss pole. The heart-shaped leaves gently curl around the support, whilst the aerial roots help to anchor the climbing stem. The plant can also be trained up a trellis, or trailed from a trough, bowl or hanging basket. It is usually happy growing at lower light intensities, so is suitable for many locations. However, this plant cannot tolerate drying out. It has thin leaves, which lose water rapidly, and once it wilts the chances of recovery are poor. The compost must therefore be kept evenly moist at all times.

COMMON NAME
Creeping Fig

Plant type	Foliage plant with climbing, creeping and trailing habit
Season of interest	All year round
Size	100–350cm (39–137in)
Flower	None
Leaf	Heart-shaped, 1.25–2.5cm ($\frac{1}{2}$–1in), slightly crinkled, mid green
Temperature	15–20°C (60–68°F)
Aspect/Light	Moderate to lightly shaded situation
Humidity	Moderate to high
Watering	Keep compost evenly moist throughout year; do not allow to dry out
Feeding	Once every two to four weeks in spring and summer
Propagation	Plant 7.5–10cm (3–4in) tip or stem cuttings with lower leaves removed in seed and cutting compost in spring to early autumn at 18–20°C (65–68°F)
Potting	Houseplant potting compost
Problems	Red spider mite, dehydration of foliage and loss of plant if allowed to dry out
Availability	Commonly available throughout year
Uses	Grow in container in slightly shaded position; can be used as trailer or trained up moss pole or trellis, where it will provide wall cover
Other varieties	F. p. 'Variegata' – cream variegation

When planting stem cuttings, take care to insert them the correct way up

Grevillea robusta

An attractive plant with ornamental, fern-like foliage, which has a brownish tinge and a slightly downy texture when young. The Grevillea is quite hardy and can be grown easily in a range of conditions. It does, however, prefer to be kept on the cool side, as higher temperatures cause lower humidity, which can lead to dehydration of the leaves. The Grevillea is therefore ideally suited to a porch. In its natural habitat this plant is a vigorous tree, so indoor specimens need to be kept in check. Unbalanced or wayward growth should be carefully trimmed off with a sharp pair of secateurs. It is also essential to maintain an erect habit, and it may be necessary to use a stake for this purpose.

COMMON NAME
Silk Oak

Plant type	Foliage plant with erect habit
Season of interest	All year round
Size	100–250cm (39–98in)
Flower	None indoors
Leaf	Fern-like, 20–40cm (8–16in), green with slight brown coloration when young
Temperature	10–18°C (50–65°F)
Aspect/Light	Moderate to full light
Humidity	Moderate
Watering	Evenly moisten compost in spring and summer, allowing to dry a little before re-watering; water less in autumn and winter
Feeding	Once every two to three weeks with houseplant fertilizer in spring and summer, when growing actively
Propagation	Sow seed at 15°C (60°F) in seed and cutting compost in spring
Potting	Houseplant potting compost
Problems	Dehydration from warm, dry atmosphere
Availability	Occasionally available, especially in spring and summer
Uses	Grow in container in cool, well-lit conservatory, either on its own or as part of group display

A stake will keep the plant erect

Hedera canariensis 'Variegata'

This boldly variegated and large-leaved ivy can be used effectively in a very wide range of situations, although it does not like hot, dry conditions. Apart from dehydration due to a dry atmosphere, it is particularly susceptible to attack by red spider mite, a pest that thrives under such conditions. The Hedera is best grown in a conservatory with a moderate temperature and full light. It can also be grown quite successfully outside, although it does not like a very exposed situation. Although the plant is occasionally grown in a mixed arrangement, it is best planted either on its own or with two or three plants of the same variety to create a more dense effect. Wire ties or rings and a bamboo cane should be used to provide support, and the plant should be trimmed occasionally with vine scissors to keep it tidy.

COMMON NAME
Canary Island Ivy

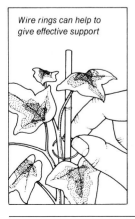

Wire rings can help to give effective support

Plant type	Foliage plant with vigorous climbing and trailing habit
Season of interest	All year round
Size	100–400cm (39–156in)
Flower	None
Leaf	Unevenly shaped, cupped, 7.5–10cm (3–4in), boldly variegated cream, white and green with red leaf stems
Temperature	7–18°C (45–65°F)
Aspect/Light	Full light
Humidity	Moderate
Watering	Evenly moisten compost in spring and summer, allowing to dry out a little between waterings; keep on drier side in autumn and winter
Feeding	Once every two to three weeks with houseplant fertilizer in spring and summer
Propagation	Plant 10–12.5cm (4–5in) tip or stem cuttings in seed and cutting or potting compost at 18–20°C (65–68°F) from mid spring to late summer
Potting	Houseplant potting compost
Problems	Red spider mite, aphid, mealy bug, root mealy bug
Availability	Commonly available throughout year
Uses	Grow in container or conservatory bed in cool, well-lit and well-ventilated conservatory; can be used in mixed planting when small, then displayed on its own as wall-trained plant

Laurus nobilis

The elegant Laurus should really be grown alternately indoors and outdoors as the season dictates. During spring and summer the plant will grow quite happily outside, and is particularly good as a specimen plant in a container on a patio or gracing the front of a house. In autumn and winter it prefers a cool to moderately heated indoor situation in full light. Although it can be grown indoors in the spring and summer, the growth can tend to become soft and etiolated. The Laurus is an excellent subject for trimming and training, the most usual shapes being the standard and pyramidal forms. Shaped plants look particularly effective when displayed in matched pairs. Remember, also, that bay leaves can be used in cooking.

COMMON NAMES
Bay Tree, Bay Laurel, Sweet Bay

Plant type	Compact foliage shrub with standard or erect habit
Season of interest	All year round
Size	100–400cm (39–156in)
Flower	Insignificant, pale greenish, produced in spring
Leaf	Oval, pointed, 5–6cm (2–2½in) long, 2–2.5 (¾–1in) wide, tough, green, with pungent smell, especially when crushed
Temperature	10–20°C (50–68°F)
Aspect/Light	Moderate to full light
Humidity	Moderate
Watering	Evenly moisten compost in spring and summer; keep on drier side when dormant in autumn and winter
Feeding	Once a month with houseplant fertilizer in spring and summer
Propagation	Plant 10cm (4in) tip cuttings with bottom leaves removed in seed and cutting compost at 18–20°C (65–68°F) from mid spring to early autumn
Potting	Houseplant potting compost
Problems	Scale insect
Availability	Commonly available as indoor or garden plant throughout year
Uses	Grow in large container (to restrain size) in cool conservatory; can also be used as patio plant

The Bay Tree can make an excellent standard plant

Maranta leuconeura erythroneura

Also known by the latin name *M. tricolor*, this is a highly attractive plant but tends to be rather delicate. Unless it can be provided with a humid, draught-free situation at an even temperature, it may be better to try the easier-to-grow variety, *M. l. kerchoviana*, first. However, if you really are keen to cultivate the plant, then put it in a terrarium or some other partly enclosed container, which will improve the humidity, whilst being adequately ventilated. The humidity can be increased still further by grouping the plant in the container with other low-growing and possibly slightly taller subjects. This Maranta does not benefit much from being misted, as this can cause spotting of the foliage.

COMMON NAMES
Herringbone Plant, Red Herringbone

Planting in a terrarium may help the plant to grow better

Plant type	Foliage plant with semi-prostrate habit
Season of interest	All year round
Size	20–25cm (8–10in)
Flower	Insignificant pale pink flowers on green spike amongst foliage, produced in spring/summer
Leaf	Oval, 10–12.5cm (4–5in) long, 5–6cm (2–2½in) wide, with two-tone green patterning, distinctive red central and lateral ribs, and pink underside
Temperature	18–21°C (65–70°F)
Aspect/Light	Moderate to slight shade
Humidity	High
Watering	Evenly moisten compost in spring and summer; keep slightly drier in autumn and winter
Feeding	Once every two to four weeks with houseplant fertilizer in spring and summer
Propagation	Divide mature plant from mid to late spring; plant 10cm (4in) cuttings in seed and cutting compost at 21°C (70°F) from early to mid summer
Potting	Houseplant potting compost
Problems	Red spider mite, mealy bug, browning of leaves due to dry atmosphere
Availability	Commonly available throughout the year
Uses	Grow in container in draught-free position in very humid conservatory; effective in mixed planting

Monstera deliciosa

The Monstera is one of the most popular and distinctive indoor plants. Unlike most other plants it grows sideways in one direction. As it grows the leaves become larger and, if conditions are right, increasingly perforated. When a new leaf unfurls it is rather like watching a cut paper pattern unfolding. At this stage the leaf is very delicate and easily damaged but in a few days it becomes stiffer and takes on the characteristic leathery texture. Failure to provide sufficient humidity results in leaves that have fewer perforations or even no holes at all. Another feature of the plant is its aerial roots, which sometimes dangle uselessly over the side. When this happens, either push them back into the compost or wind them round the stem.

COMMON NAMES
Swiss Cheese Plant,
Mexican Breadfruit Plant

Plant type	Foliage plant with lateral growth
Season of interest	All year round
Size	100–400cm (39–156in) with similar spread
Flower	Occasional, greenish white, arum-like spathe on mature plant, followed by development of whitish fruit from spadix, produced at almost any time
Leaf	Heart-shaped when young, developing perforations and cuts, 10–45cm (4–18in) long, 10–45cm (4–18in) wide, leathery, green, on rigid stems
Temperature	18–21°C (65–70°F)
Aspect/Light	Well-lit situation, but out of direct sun
Humidity	Moderate to high
Watering	Evenly moisten compost in spring and summer, allowing to dry a little before re-watering; keep on drier side in autumn and winter
Feeding	Once every two to three weeks with houseplant fertilizer in spring and summer
Propagation	Plant growing point with three leaves supported with cane at 21°C (70°F) in potting compost in mid spring to early summer; sow seeds in seed and cutting compost at 21–24°C (70–75°F)
Potting	Houseplant potting compost
Availability	Commonly available throughout year
Uses	Grow at floor level in large container or plant in conservatory bed

Aerial roots may be wound loosely around the plant

Pelargonium tomentosum

This Pelargonium produces small, pale blue flowers but the main interest of the plant lies in its aromatic foliage. The distinctive peppermint scent is released when the leaves are crushed and also naturally in the late evening, particularly following a hot, sunny day. If space is limited in the conservatory in summer, Pelargoniums can be grown as patio plants and moved back under cover in the early autumn. They will usually maintain their foliage and its scent all year round. This variety is useful as a background to more colourful foliage plants. Other aromatic Pelargoniums include *P. fragrans*, with nutmeg-scented leaves, and *P.* 'Prince of Orange', with orange-scented foliage.

COMMON NAMES
Pelargonium, Peppermint-scented Geranium

Take cuttings that are three leaf joints long and remove the lower two pairs of leaves

Plant type	Foliage plant with upright habit
Season of interest	All year round, especially late spring to early autumn
Size	Up to 100cm (39in) in height and spread
Flower	Small, pale blue
Leaf	Hand-shaped and further divided, 5cm (2in) wide, grey-green, peppermint scented
Temperature	0–20°C (32–68°F)
Aspect/Light	Will tolerate light shade but prefers a bright situation, which will also help to release the leaf scent
Humidity	Average
Watering	Keep compost evenly moist in spring and summer; water less in autumn and winter
Feeding	Once every week with liquid houseplant fertilizer from late spring to early autumn
Propagation	Root softwood cuttings in seed and cutting compost at 15–18°C (60–65°F)
Potting	Houseplant or general potting compost
Problems	Vine weevil, mealy bug, red spider mite
Availability	Quite commonly available from spring to summer
Uses	Grow in container, either on its own or as part of group

Persea americana

Although it is rarely available to buy as a plant, the Persea can be grown from the stone found inside the Avocado fruit. The stone can either be planted in seed and cutting compost or suspended over a tumbler of water with the broadest part just in contact with the surface of the water. Various methods can be employed to support the stone, such as matchsticks pushed into the skin, or looped wire, and many kitchen windowsills are often occupied by the experiment. The Persea has a rather spindly habit of growth and the plant takes up a fair amount of space, as might be expected of a species which in its natural environment grows to tree size. However, the plant's height makes it useful for mixed plantings.

COMMON NAME
Avocado Pear

Plant type	Foliage plant with erect habit
Season of interest	All year round
Size	100–300cm (39–117in)
Flower	Usually none as houseplant
Leaf	Oval, 7.5–12.5cm (3–5in) long, 5–7.5cm (2–3in) wide, green
Temperature	18–21°C (64–70°F)
Aspect/Light	Well-lit situation with sunlight
Humidity	Moderate
Watering	Evenly moisten compost in spring and summer; keep on drier side when dormant in autumn and winter
Feeding	Once every two to three weeks with houseplant fertilizer in spring and summer
Propagation	From Avocado Pear stone suspended over water or planted, with one third of stone exposed, in seed and cutting compost at 21°C (70°F)
Potting	Houseplant potting compost
Problems	Mealy bug, scale insect, premature lower leaf loss from over-watering
Availability	Rarely commercially available as plant; usually grown from Avocado Pear stone
Uses	Grow at floor-level in well-lit position in heated conservatory; gives height to mixed displays

An Avocado Pear stone can be germinated by suspending it over water

Petroselinum crispum

Parsley is one of the most useful of all the culinary herbs, and though it is really happier outside it can also be grown in pots in the cool conservatory, where the growing season may be extended. The main problem with Parsley is the length of time taken for the seed to germinate. It can be sown at any time from early spring to mid summer, and germination may be speeded up if boiling water is poured on the soil before the seed is sown. Parsley will flourish in either full sun or partial shade, but requires a plentiful supply of moisture to do well. It is a biennial plant, flowering in the summer of its second year of growth, though it is most satisfactory to propagate new plants from seed each year.

COMMON NAME
Parsley

Plant type	Foliage plant with bushy habit
Season of interest	Late spring to autumn
Size	15–22.5cm (6–9in)
Flower	Small, white, in clusters
Leaf	Curled and deeply divided, mid-green, edible
Temperature	Minimum −2°C (28°F)
Aspect/Light	Full sun to light shade
Humidity	Moderate
Watering	Keep compost evenly moist throughout growing season
Feeding	Not normally needed
Propagation	Sow seed in seed and cutting compost at 19–24°C (66–75°F) from early spring to mid summer
Potting	Houseplant potting compost
Problems	Slow to germinate
Availability	Commonly available as seed from early winter onwards; or as pre-grown plants from early spring to late summer
Uses	Grow in container or conservatory bed, either on its own or mixed with other plants

Sow several groups of seeds in threes to achieve bushy growth

Philodendron scandens

This Philodendron can be a vigorous climber. Although the plant has relatively feeble stems, it can produce quite strong growth once adequately supported. It grows particularly well when trained up a wall. However, provided care is taken not to allow the roots growing in the compost to suffer in any way, this plant can also be supported by no more than a bamboo cane, with wire rings looped around the stem. Although the leaves may initially look untidy as they are bent out of place, many will grow to face tidily outwards as they adapt to the direction of the light.

COMMON NAME
Sweetheart Plant

Plant type	Foliage plant with climbing habit
Season of interest	All year round
Size	60–250cm (24–98in)
Flower	None
Leaf	Heart-shaped, 5–7.5cm (2–3in), green
Temperature	16–21°C (61–70°F)
Aspect/Light	Moderate light, but will tolerate a little shade
Humidity	Moderate to high
Watering	Evenly moisten compost in spring and summer but do not over-water; keep drier in autumn and winter
Feeding	Once every two to four weeks with houseplant fertilizer in spring and summer
Propagation	Plant tip cuttings, 7.5–10cm (3–4in), in seed and cutting compost at 21°C (70°F) in mid spring to early autumn
Potting	Houseplant potting compost
Problems	Mealy bug, root rot from over-watering
Availability	Commonly available throughout year
Uses	Grow in conservatory bed or large container and train up wall; can also be grown in body of room with support
Other varieties	*P. hastatum* – larger and more angular; longer green leaves

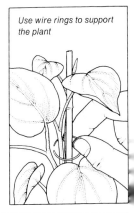

Use wire rings to support the plant

Phormium tenax

The sword-shaped leaves of the Phormium make a bold display in a group of conservatory shrubs. There are a number of striking cultivars available with brightly coloured and variegated leaves, many of which are smaller in size. They include *P. t.* 'Purpureum', which has bronze-purple foliage, and *P. t.* 'Variegatum', with green and yellow striped leaves.

Although the Phormium is grown mainly for its foliage, it also has large panicles of dark red flowers in summer, borne on tall stems, which are followed by orange seed heads.

COMMON NAME
New Zealand Flax

Plant type	Foliage plant with tufted habit
Season of interest	All year
Size	30–180cm (12–72in)
Flower	Dark red, 10cm (2in) long, borne in panicles on long flower stems, followed by orange seed heads
Leaf	Sword-shaped, erect and slightly arched, to 180cm (72in) long, dark-green, bronze, purple, variegated
Temperature	-3–16°C (26–61°F)
Aspect/Light	Full sun
Humidity	Moderate
Watering	As required; do not over water
Propagation	Divide established plants in spring
Potting	Houseplant potting compost
Problems	Large plants may burst plastic, earthenware or wooden containers
Availability	Commonly available from mid spring to midsummer
Uses	Grow in large container or conservatory bed, either on its own or in mixed planting

Divide and re-pot the plant every 5 years to avoid damage to pots from the strong roots

Pleomele reflexa variegata

The Pleomele is very rarely seen nowadays, although it really is quite a choice plant. The green and yellow-green variegated foliage is attractive and becomes more interesting as the erect habit turns a little more wayward and starts to grow horizontally or in a semi-erect fashion. As this happens, it is advisable to provide the plant with some support using bamboo cane and wire rings. The plant requires a fairly high level of humidity, which can be provided by regular misting or by standing the pot in a tray of moist pebbles. The Pleomele is quite slow-growing, which means that it takes a considerable time to produce a plant of worthy proportions to display effectively.

COMMON NAME
Song of India

Plant type	Foliage plant with erect, then semi-erect, habit
Season of interest	All year round
Size	100–300cm (39–117in)
Flower	None
Leaf	Lance-like, 10–20cm (4–8in) long, 2–2.5cm ($\frac{3}{4}$–1in) wide, green and yellow-green striped
Temperature	18–21°C (64–70°F)
Aspect/Light	Well-lit situation, but out of direct sunlight
Humidity	Moderate to high
Watering	Evenly moisten compost throughout year, taking care not to over-water and allowing to dry out a little before re-watering
Feeding	Once every three to four weeks with houseplant fertilizer in spring and summer
Propagation	Plant 10cm (4in) tip cuttings in seed and cutting compost at 21°C (70°F) in early spring
Potting	Houseplant potting compost
Problems	Mealy bug, leaf loss from over-watering
Availability	Rarely available
Uses	Grow in container and display on its own in prominent position

Wayward growth may need some support to prevent damage

Sansevieria trifasciata 'Laurentii'

The Sansevieria has been a popular plant for some time, and it must be one of the easiest to look after, provided that it is grown in full light and not over-watered. It can tolerate slightly less well-lit conditions, although its leaf colour and habit may change. Whilst the plant can be propagated from sections of leaf, the golden-yellow edged variegation may be lost by this technique. It is therefore better to propagate by cutting off offshoots at the base, and separating a piece of the rhizome with the new shoot, as this preserves the true colour. The plant prefers to be grown in a container that is just large enough for it, but it is advisable to check the rate of growth from time to time, as the roots are capable of breaking a pot.

COMMON NAME
Mother-in-law's Tongue

Propagation is best achieved by separating the plant

Plant type	Semi-succulent foliage plant with erect habit
Season of interest	All year round
Size	45–90cm (18–36in)
Flower	30cm (1ft) spike of small, greenish white, delicately scented flowers, produced in late spring/summer
Leaf	Erect, strap-like, pointed, 30–90cm (12–36in), cream-bordered with light and dark green patterned middle
Temperature	13–28°C (55–82°F)
Aspect/Light	Full sun
Humidity	Low
Watering	Evenly moisten compost in spring and summer, allowing to dry a little before re-watering; keep on dry side in autumn and winter
Feeding	Once every three to four weeks with half strength flowering plant fertilizer in spring and summer
Propagation	Cut out 20cm (8in) offshoots, with rhizome, in late spring to mid summer and pot in cactus and succulent compost at 20–22°C (68–72°F)
Potting	Cactus and succulent compost or houseplant potting compost
Problems	Mealy bug, aphid (on flower spike), root and stem rot when over-moist or cold
Availability	Commonly available throughout year
Uses	Grow in container and display on its own or in groups

Syngonium podophyllum

A vigorous plant that undergoes quite dramatic changes in habit and leaf shape as it grows. When young it produces arrow-shaped leaves on erect stems. As it gets older, though, the plant produces leaves that are divided into sections on stems which climb and semi-trail. The Syngonium is often featured in bowl plantings, but will quickly get out of control, so is best used on its own, with either a moss pole or a trellis for support. Because of its untidy habit, this plant is not as popular as the variety *S. p.* 'Emerald Gem'. This has more attractively coloured and shaped foliage, is slower-growing and smaller and more compact in stature.

COMMON NAMES
Arrowhead Plant, African Evergreen

Plant type	Foliage plant with climbing habit that can trail
Season of interest	All year round
Size	100–200cm (39–78in)
Flower	Unlikely indoors
Leaf	Arrow-shaped on young plants, divided into sections as plant matures, 10–30cm (4–12in) long, 5–12.5cm (2–5in) wide, green
Temperature	13–19°C (55–66°F)
Aspect/Light	Well-lit situation, but out of direct sun
Humidity	Moderate to high
Watering	Evenly moisten compost in spring and summer, allowing to dry a little before re-watering; keep drier in autumn and winter
Feeding	Once every two to four weeks with houseplant fertilizer in spring and summer
Propagation	Plant 7.5–10cm (3–4in) tip cuttings in seed and cutting compost at 20–21°C (68–70°F)
Potting	Houseplant potting compost
Problems	Aphid, mealy bug
Availability	Commonly available throughout year
Uses	Grow in container or conservatory bed and train up moss poll or trellis; prefers cool conservatory
Other varieties	*S.p.* 'Emerald Gem' – light and dark green leaves; smaller and more compact

A moss pole provides effective support

Adiantum capillus-veneris

An attractive little plant with delicate, pale green, fan-shaped fronds. The Adiantum is a versatile fern that can either be displayed on its own or used to add softness to a mixed planting. The main problem with the plant is that it is very susceptible to dehydration. If the compost becomes too dry or the humidity is not kept high enough, the thin fronds quickly wither and die. Plants that have suffered dehydration can sometimes be saved if remedial action is taken early enough. The shrivelled fronds may even become turgid again, but it is usually necessary to cut them off just above soil level, using sharp scissors. Associated planting will of course provide the plant with a more humid atmosphere.

COMMON NAME
Maidenhair Fern

Regularly check the compost to ensure that it is kept moist

Plant type	Fern with bushy, multi-stemmed, compact habit
Season of interest	All year round
Size	20–30cm (8–12in)
Flower	None
Leaf	Fan-shaped fronds, 20–30cm (8–12in), serrated, mid-green leaflets on brown to blackish stems
Temperature	16–20°C (60–68°F)
Aspect/Light	Moderate light, but out of direct sunlight
Humidity	Moderate to high; dislikes dry atmosphere
Watering	Keep compost evenly moist throughout year
Feeding	Once every three to four weeks with half strength houseplant fertilizer in spring and summer
Propagation	Divide plant into clumps in spring or summer and pot singly
Potting	Seed and cutting compost, or mixture of potting compost and medium to coarse sphagnum moss peat
Problems	Dehydration due to dry atmosphere or to compost drying out
Availability	Commonly available throughout the year
Uses	Grow in container in body of conservatory; provides useful foliage foil for mixed displays
Other varieties	*A. raddianum* – more incised leaflets

Asplenium nidus

A beautiful fern with bright green, undulating fronds that are held in an upward-spreading rosette. The young fronds slowly unfurl from the centre, and have a soft, shiny texture. They are very delicate and should not be handled for the first few weeks. Mature fronds develop brown parallel lines on the underside, which later produce dust-like spores. The spores can be collected and used to propagate new plants. Although the Asplenium is often used in bowl gardens and mixed planters, it can quickly be overcome by more vigorous plants, so is best grown singly as a feature plant. A constant watch should be kept for scale insects, which can be difficult to control as the plant is sensitive to many spray chemicals. The safest way to deal with minor infestations is to simply remove the insects with a fingernail.

COMMON NAME
Birds-nest Fern

Plant type	Fern with upright habit
Season of interest	All year round
Size	30–75cm (12–18in)
Flower	None
Leaf	Tongue shaped fronds, 15–75cm (8–30in) long, 5–10cm (2–4in) across, bright green, arranged in rosette with brown central rib
Temperature	16–21°C (61–70°F)
Aspect/Light	Moderate light
Humidity	Moderate to high
Watering	Keep compost evenly moist in spring and summer; water a little less in autumn and winter, but do not allow compost to dry out
Feeding	Once every three to four weeks with half strength houseplant fertilizer in spring and summer
Propagation	Collect spores and scatter in pans or trays of seed and cutting compost at 21°C (70°F) in spring or summer; when large enough to handle, pot up singly
Potting	Houseplant potting compost
Problems	Scale insect, aphid, browning of fronds due to dry atmosphere
Availability	Quite commonly available throughout year
Uses	Grow in container in conservatory that is humid but not too warm; prefers position that is fairly well lit but away from draughts; display on its own

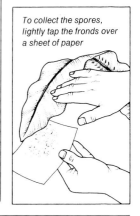

To collect the spores, lightly tap the fronds over a sheet of paper

An extraordinary plant with strange-looking fronds and a lop-sided habit of growth. The Platycerium produces two types of frond: sterile, shield-shaped fronds, which anchor the plant to its support; and fertile, antler-like fronds. The plant can either be grown in a hanging pot or basket or attached to a piece of cork bark and hung on a wall. Cover the root ball with a mixture of sphagnum moss and sphagnum moss peat, and attach the sterile fronds to the bark using plastic coated wire. Water the plant by either spraying the moss or immersing it in water for a few minutes.

COMMON NAME
Stag's Horn Fern

Plant type	Fern with unusual prostrate habit
Season of interest	All year round
Size	15–120cm (6–48in)
Flower	None
Leaf	Two distinct frond types: sterile frond at base of plant and wrapped around support; fertile frond prominent, antler-like, 30–90cm (1–3ft) long, green
Temperature	18–24°C (64–75°F)
Aspect/Light	Moderate to reasonable light, but away from direct sunlight
Humidity	Moderate to high
Watering	Evenly moisten compost throughout year, allowing to dry just a little before re-watering
Feeding	Once every four to six weeks with half strength houseplant fertilizer in spring and summer
Propagation	Collect spores from underside of fertile fronds and scatter on seed and cutting compost at 21°C (70°F) in spring and early summer
Potting	Mixture of sphagnum moss, peat and bark
Problems	Scale insect
Availability	Occasionally available throughout year
Uses	Grow on its own or in twos or threes in hanging basket or pot or attached to cork bark hung from wall

The Platycerium can be grown on a piece of cork bark

Phoenix canariensis

A distinctive and extremely attractive palm, with stiff leaflets and an upright but spreading habit. When it is small and fairly compact it makes a good plant for table-top display. As it grows taller and the branches spread, the Phoenix is best moved down to the floor. It is important to maintain a high level of humidity otherwise the leaflets will quickly turn brown at the ends and require trimming. If this becomes necessary, use sharp scissors and leave a thin edge of dead tissue. When the Phoenix produces new fronds, the leaflets tend to stick together as they emerge. These will normally free themselves as they grow, but if they begin to suffer tease them gently apart.

COMMON NAMES
Canary Date Palm, Canary Islands Date Palm, Feather Palm

Plant type	Palm with erect but spreading habit
Season of interest	All year round
Size	100–300cm (39–117in)
Flower	None indoors
Leaf	Feather-like fronds 30–100cm (12–39in) long, comprised of many stiff leaflets, 10–20cm (4–8in) long, 0.5–1cm ($\frac{1}{4}$–$\frac{1}{2}$in) wide, green
Temperature	18–21°C (64–70°F)
Aspect/Light	Well-lit situation with some sunlight
Humidity	Moderate to high
Watering	Evenly moisten compost in spring and summer, allowing to dry just a little before re-watering; water less in autumn and winter
Feeding	Once every two to four weeks with houseplant fertilizer in spring and summer
Propagation	Sow seeds in seed and cutting compost at 27°C (80°F) in mid to late spring
Potting	Houseplant potting compost
Problems	Mealy bug, root mealy bug, scale insect, root rot due to over-watering, browning of leaves in dry atmosphere
Availability	Occasionally available throughout year
Uses	Grow in container and use either on its own or to provide height in mixed planting
Other varieties	P. dactylifera – more upright and vigorous

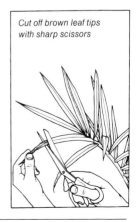

Cut off brown leaf tips with sharp scissors

Trachycarpus fortunei

This evergreen palm with large fan-shaped leaves grows well in a large container and makes a good feature shrub for the conservatory. The pleated leaves, up to 90cm (36in) wide, are borne on strong, dark green leaf stalks clustered at the summit of a tall, rough, brown trunk. An individual leaf will remain on the plant for many years before it starts to discolour with age. The Trachycarpus also produces long panicles of small yellow flowers in early summer, which are followed by round blue-black fruits. No pruning is necessary apart from the occasional removal of old and damaged leaves.

COMMON NAME
Windmill Palm

Remove old or dying lower leaves to improve the plant's appearance

Plant type	Palm with upright habit
Season of interest	All year round
Size	To 100–200cm (72–96in) when grown in a pot, if not double
Flower	Small, yellow, borne in panicles 60cm (24in) long
Leaf	Large, fan-shaped, to 90cm (36in) wide and 60cm (24in) long, mid-green, on long leaf-stalk.
Temperature	4–7°C (40–45°F)
Aspect/Light	Well-lit situation with exposure to direct sunlight
Humidity	Moderate
Watering	Keep compost evenly moist from spring to autumn; keep on drier side in winter
Feeding	Once every two weeks with houseplant fertilizer during summer growing period
Propagation	Sow seeds in seed and cutting compost at 24°C (75°F) in early spring
Potting	Soil-based potting compost
Problems	Overall size of leaves
Availability	Sometimes scarce
Uses	Grow in large container and display on its own

Washingtonia filifera

An extraordinary palm with large, fan-like fronds and brown, fibrous threads hanging from the end of each leaflet. It is not often seen for sale, perhaps because the habit of growth is too wide for many locations in the conservatory.

As with most palms, the key to effective care is careful watering. The compost should be evenly moistened but should also be allowed to dry a little between waterings to prevent the roots from rotting. A high level of humidity is also important otherwise the leaf tips turn brown. Unlike most other palms it is not possible to trim the leaves without ruining the appearance of the plant, as the characteristic wispy threads will obviously be lost in the process.

COMMON NAMES
Washington Palm, Desert Fan Palm, Petticoat Palm

Plant type	Palm with erect but spreading habit
Season of interest	All year round
Size	100–250cm (39–98in)
Flower	None indoors
Leaf	Fan-shaped fronds, 45–60cm (18–24in) across, comprised of leaflets, 15–45cm (6–18in) long, 1–2.5cm ($\frac{1}{2}$–1in) wide, stiff, green, with wispy brown fibres hanging from the ends; leaflets radiate from 30–45cm (12–18in) stalk
Temperature	18–21°C (64–70°F)
Aspect/Light	Well-lit situation with some sunlight
Humidity	Moderate
Watering	Evenly moisten compost in spring and summer, taking care not to over-water, and allowing to dry a little before re-watering; water just enough to prevent drying out in autumn and winter
Feeding	Once every two to four weeks with houseplant fertilizer in spring and summer
Propagation	Sow seeds in seed and cutting compost at 27°C (80°F) in mid to late spring
Potting	Houseplant potting compost
Problems	Mealy bug, root mealy bug, scale insect, root rot due to over-watering, browning of leaf tips in dry atmosphere
Availability	Not often available
Uses	Grow at floor level in large container

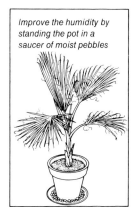

Improve the humidity by standing the pot in a saucer of moist pebbles

Abutilon × hybridum

Saucer-shaped flowers, which closely resemble those of the Hibiscus, are the main attraction of this showy shrub. It is also worth growing for its handsome three-or-five lobed leaves, which are sometimes variegated. Their shape gives the plant its common name of Flowering Maple. Colourful varieties include 'Ashford Red', 'Boule de Neige' (white), 'Canary Bird' (yellow), and 'Kentish Belle' (bronze or copper). *A. striatum thompsonii* has variegated green and yellow leaves. Abutilons can grow quite large, so are most suitable for the conservatory, where they may be planted in a border or pot-grown. Pot-grown specimens will appreciate being stood outside in summer. These shrubs are quite easy to grow, but can become leggy if not pruned. Cut them back hard in autumn to encourage shapely growth.

COMMON NAME
Flowering Maple

Water large plants through a hollow tube to ensure the roots get water

Plant type	Flowering shrub with upright habit
Season of interest	Early summer to autumn
Size	To 180cm (72in)
Flower	Saucer-shaped, 5cm (2in), red, yellow, white or pink
Leaf	7.5cm (3in), 3–5 lobed, maple- shaped, green or variegated
Temperature	10–20°C (50–60°F)
Aspect/Light	Well-lit situation with some exposure to sunlight
Humidity	Moderate
Watering	Evenly moisten compost from spring to autumn; keep drier in winter
Feeding	Liquid plant fertilizer once every two weeks in spring and early summer
Propagation	Plant 10–15cm (4–6in) stem cuttings in seed and cutting compost at 15–18°C (59–64°F) in summer; sow seeds in seed and cutting compost at 15–18°C (59–64°F) in late winter
Potting	Potting compost
Problems	Mealy bug, aphid, rate of growth and overall size
Availability	Commonly available throughout the year
Uses	Grow in container or conservatory bed; provides height in mixed display
Other varieties	A. × h. *savitzii* – leaves variegated green and white

Abutilon megapotamicum 'Variegatum'

Although rather a leggy subject, the Abutilon can be made to look quite attractive if it is trimmed in early spring and provided with a light framework of canes or some other form of support. The loose habit of growth is enhanced by the hanging, bell-shaped flowers. However, the thin leaves are quite frail and the plant is susceptible to dehydration if the air is too dry, resulting in loss of foliage and occasionally the entire plant. The Abutilon requires a sunny position – failure to provide sufficient light will result in a lack of flowers and drab foliage. A container-grown plant will remain attractive for two to three years before becoming unkempt. If it is then planted in a conservatory bed, the plant will gain a new lease of life.

COMMON NAME
Trailing Abutilon

Plant type	Flowering plant with loose, leggy, trailing habit that can be trained with support
Season of interest	Spring to summer
Size	30–60cm (12–24in)
Flower	Pendulous, bell-shaped, yellow and red, growing from leaf axils
Leaf	Elongated heart shaped, serrated, thin, 5–10cm (2–4in), green with occasional yellow spots
Temperature	18–21°C (65–70°F)
Aspect/Light	Well-lit situation
Humidity	Average, but dislikes excessively dry air, which can cause the leaves to shrivel
Watering	Evenly moisten compost in spring and summer; keep on dry side in autumn and winter
Feeding	Once every two to three weeks with flowering plant fertilizer in spring and summer
Propagation	Plant 7.5–10cm (3–4in) tip cuttings at 20–21°C (68–70°F) in mid spring to early summer
Potting	Potting compost
Problems	Red spider mite, scale insect
Availability	Late spring to early summer; infrequently available
Uses	Grow in container or conservatory bed; prefers sunny position
Other varieties	*A. megapotamicum* – plain green leaves; trailing habit

A light framework will help to support the plant

Acacia armata

This Australian flowering shrub is the Mimosa seen in florists' shops. The Acacia deserves a place in the conservatory for the yellow, fluffy flowers, often sweetly scented, which appear in late winter and early spring. Year round interest is maintained by the evergreen, fern-like, bright green foliage. There are a number of other varieties available: *A. dealbata* has silvery foliage, as does *A. podalyriifolia*, the Queensland Wattle. Acacias grow fast and need plenty of space for their spreading branches. They should be cut back after flowering if growth needs to be controlled. Though watering should be reduced in winter, it is important not to let the compost dry completely, as the flower buds may drop before opening.

COMMON NAMES
Kangaroo Thorn, Wattle

Plant type	Flowering shrub with upright habit
Season of interest	Late winter to early summer
Size	3m (10ft) when grown in a pot, if not double
Flower	Rounded, fluffy, 1.25cm (½in), bright yellow
Leaf	Narrow, spiny or pinnate, fern-like, 2.5cm (1in), dark or silvery green
Temperature	7–18°C (45–64°F)
Aspect/Light	Well-lit situation with exposure to sunlight
Humidity	Medium to dry
Watering	Evenly moisten compost from spring to autumn; reduce water in winter but do not allow to dry out completely
Feeding	Once every two weeks with flowering plant fertilizer in spring and early summer
Propagation	Plant 10cm (4in) stem cuttings in seed and cutting compost at 16–18°C (61–64°F) in summer; sow seeds in seed and cutting compost at 21°C (70°F) in spring
Potting	Soil-based potting compost
Problems	Flower buds drop if plant is allowed to dry out in winter
Availability	Commonly available throughout the year
Uses	Grow in container or conservatory bed, either on its own or to give height to mixed displays

Provide drainage material and keep the base of the pot off ground level

Aeschynanthus 'Mona Lisa'

This compact and low-growing Aeschynanthus is a relatively new variety. Like other trailing plants it may be used in a hanging pot or basket or displayed on a pedestal, but is perhaps better placed where the loose, somewhat straggly trails can lay almost semi-prostrate. It is particularly effective when grown in a bowl or trough where it associates well with many other plants. Position the Aeschynanthus at the front of the arrangement where the contrasting dark green leaves and reddish orange flowers can be seen to best effect.

Plant type	Flowering plant with loose, trailing habit
Season of interest	Summer
Size	10–15cm (4–6in) high, 20–40cm (8–16in) trails
Flower	Tube-like, 5–6cm (2–2½in) long, reddish orange
Leaf	Pointed oval, glossy, dark green, 5cm (2in) long
Temperature	15–21°C (59–70°F)
Aspect/Light	Well-lit situation, out of direct sunlight
Humidity	High
Watering	Keep compost evenly moist in summer when plant is in flower; allow to dry a little between waterings at other times
Feeding	Half strength flowering plant fertilizer every three to four weeks in spring and summer
Propagation	Plant 7.5–10cm (3–4in) tip or stem cuttings in seed and cutting compost at 21°C (70°F) in spring and summer
Potting	Houseplant potting compost
Problems	Mealy bug, aphid
Availability	Occasionally available late spring to early summer
Uses	Grow in container in prominent position

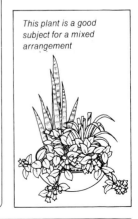

This plant is a good subject for a mixed arrangement

Allamanda cathartica

Surprisingly, perhaps, the Allamanda is not usually considered a climbing plant, but more a bushy shrub. However, the plant is really at its best if allowed to climb and provided with a means of support such as a light frame, bamboo canes, a trellis or wires attached to the wall. It therefore makes an ideal plant for the conservatory, where there is usually the space for it to climb and for the shrubby habit to develop to best effect. Without occasional trimming or pruning, the Allamanda can easily become rather straggly and untidy. When this happens it may be worth pruning back the growth by a half to two thirds in the latter part of winter before fresh growth starts. A less vigorous and more compact variety is *A.c.* 'Grandiflora'.

COMMON NAME
Golden Trumpet

A light frame can provide effective support

Plant type	Flowering plant with bushy semi-trailing habit
Season of interest	Summer
Size	60–400cm (24–156in)
Flower	Trumpet-shaped, formed by five petals, 5–10cm (2–4in) wide, golden-yellow
Leaf	Oval, 7.5–12.5cm (3–5in) long, dark green
Temperature	18–21°C (64–70°F)
Aspect/Light	Well-lit situation, without too much direct sun
Humidity	High
Watering	Evenly moisten compost in spring and summer, allowing to dry just a little before re-watering; keep on drier side in autumn and winter
Feeding	Once every three to four weeks with flowering plant fertilizer in spring and summer
Propagation	Plant 7.5–10cm (3–4in) tip cuttings in seed and cutting compost at 21–22°C (70–72°F) in mid spring to early summer
Potting	Houseplant and potting compost
Problems	Aphid, red spider mite
Availability	Occasionally available in early summer
Uses	Grow in container or conservatory bed and train up trellis or similar support
Other varieties	*A.c.* 'Grandiflora' – more compact habit

Anisodontea halvastrum

Many members of the Mallow family adorn our gardens but this tender plant from the South Island of New Zealand requires the protection of a conservatory if it is to survive. Ideal for growing in a pot, the Anisodontea has an erect habit, evergreen foliage and rosy-magenta, mallow-shaped flowers, which are produced at each leaf-joint either singly or in threes. The flowering period lasts from spring until autumn. This is a versatile plant, which is suitable for growing singly or in a mixed planting with foliage plants. In summer, it can be moved outside and used as a patio plant if preferred.

COMMON NAME
Anisodontea

Plant type	Flowering shrub with erect habit
Season of interest	Spring to autumn
Size	Up to 100cm (39in) high, 100cm (39in) wide
Flower	Mallow-shaped, single, 2cm ($\frac{3}{4}$in) wide, pale rosy-magenta
Leaf	Ovate with lobed edges, 2–3cm ($\frac{3}{4}$in) long and wide, mid green
Temperature	0–20°C (32–68°F)
Aspect/Light	Full sun
Humidity	Average
Watering	Evenly moisten compost from late spring to early autumn; keep on dry side in winter
Feeding	Liquid houseplant fertilizer in mid spring and again in mid summer
Propagation	Root softwood cuttings in houseplant potting compost at 18–19°C (65–66°F)
Potting	General or houseplant potting compost
Problems	Vine weevil
Availability	Quite commonly available from late spring to summer
Uses	Grow in container either on its own or grouped with foliage plants

The Anisodontea can be used as a patio plant in summer

Anthurium andreanum

The most apt of this plant's common names is Painter's Palette, as it can produce flower heads in several different colours. These are white, an almost gaudy pink (the Flamingo Flower or Lily), and bright red, which is the most common form. Rather demanding in its cultural requirements, the plant requires constantly high humidity, and the aerial roots should be mulched occasionally with sphagnum moss. However, if it can be grown satisfactorily, the Anthurium will produce its bright flowers for a long period. Left on the plant the flowers will last for several weeks before they fade and deteriorate, but will need support to display them at their best. Alternatively, they can be removed for use in cut flower arrangements.

COMMON NAMES
Flamingo Flower, Flamingo Lily, Painter's Palette, Oilcloth Flower

Sphagnum moss may be used as a mulch around the aerial roots

Plant type	Flowering plant with erect, open habit
Season of interest	Usually summer, but occasionally throughout year if conditions are favourable
Size	45–100cm (18–39in)
Flower	Spathe heart-shaped, 10–12.5cm (4–5in), white, pink or red; spadix poker-like, erect, 5–7.5cm (2–3in) long, white, yellow, on 30–45cm (12–18in) stem
Leaf	Heart-shaped, 15–25cm (6–10in) long, green, on 25–30cm (10–12in) stems
Temperature	18–24°C (64–75°F)
Aspect/Light	Moderate light with some shade
Humidity	High
Watering	Keep compost evenly moist in spring and summer; allow to dry very slightly before re-watering in autumn and winter
Feeding	Once every two to four weeks with houseplant fertilizer in spring and summer
Propagation	Separate plantlets in mid spring to mid summer and put into potting compost with sphagnum moss added at 24°C (75°F); sow seeds as above
Potting	Houseplant potting compost with sphagnum moss added
Problems	Aphid, red spider mite
Availability	Occasionally available throughout year
Uses	Grow in container or conservatory bed; can be used on its own or in groups

Begonia elatior hybrids

This Begonia is a popular and highly colourful plant that can provide a showy display for a very long time, often remaining in flower for months. It can be used to brighten up planting schemes and works well with foliage plants. One of its few weaknesses is that the growth is very floppy and rather brittle. Unsupported, the stems can easily sag and snap off. One other problem with this Begonia is its susceptibility to pests and diseases. A careful check should be kept for aphid, and any fading and dead flowers should be cleanly removed to prevent infection by diseases. Old leaves and other damaged tissue should be treated similarly.

Plant type	Flowering plant with erect, busy habit
Season of interest	Spring and summer
Size	15–30cm (6–12in)
Flower	4–5cm (1½–2in), red, pink or orange
Leaf	Rounded heart-shaped with slightly serrated edge, 5–10cm (2–4in), fleshy, green, crinkled
Temperature	15–19°C (59–66°F)
Aspect/Light	Well-lit situation with some exposure to sunlight
Humidity	Moderate to high
Watering	Evenly moisten compost in spring and summer, allowing to dry a little before re-watering; keep on dry side in autumn and winter
Feeding	Once every two to three weeks with flowering plant fertilizer in spring and summer
Propagation	Plant 7.5–10cm (3–4in) tip cuttings in seed and cutting compost at 20–21°C (68–70°F) in spring and summer
Potting	Houseplant potting compost
Problems	Aphid, botrytis, mildew
Availability	Commonly available in spring and summer
Uses	Grow in container either on its own or in group backed by foliage plants

Use a light framework of sticks and twine to support the plant

Bougainvillea glabra

Despite the difficulty that may be encountered with its cultivation, the unusual and highly colourful Bougainvillea is worth all the effort. Avoid allowing the plant to dry to wilting point during the growing season, but keep it a little drier and slightly cooler for a short period in the winter. As the Bougainvillea starts to grow in the spring, the choice must be made as to whether it should be grown as a relatively loose bush, or encouraged to climb. As a climber the plant can be supported either by a bamboo cane or by a wire frame, possibly formed into a hoop. Care should be taken as the stems can produce sharp spines. It is essential to place the plant in direct sunlight, otherwise the growth becomes leggy and the flowering potential will be reduced. Aphids are strongly attracted to the Bougainvillea so make regular checks for them.

COMMON NAME
Paper Flower

Regularly train the growth to maintain a good shape

Plant type	Flowering plant with climbing habit
Season of interest	Spring and summer
Size	100–400cm (39–156in)
Flower	Small, white, amidst three 2.5–5cm (1–2in) pink or purple bracts
Leaf	Pointed oval, 5cm (2in), mid green
Temperature	16–20°C (61–68°F)
Aspect/Light	Well-lit situation with exposure to full sun
Humidity	Moderate
Watering	Evenly moisten compost in spring and summer, allowing to dry just a little before re-watering; keep on drier side in autumn and winter
Feeding	Flowering plant fertilizer once every two weeks in spring and summer
Propagation	Plant 10–15cm (4–6in) tip or stem cuttings in seed and cutting compost at 24°C (75°F) in mid spring to early summer
Potting	Houseplant potting compost
Problems	Aphid
Availability	Often available from mid spring to early summer
Uses	Grow in large container or conservatory bed and train on canes or wire frame, or up wall

Brunfelsia pauciflora calycina

The Brunfelsia's unusual common name of Yesterday, Today and Tomorrow Plant relates to the extraordinary development of the flowers. On the first day of opening they are purple in colour; by the second day they have faded to a paler blue; and by the third day they are an off-white colour. On the fourth day the flower deteriorates. The plant's erect, bushy habit can easily become rather leggy and get out of control. To maintain a more compact and balanced growth, the growing tips should be pinched out regularly and the plant should be trimmed back in the spring. The variety 'Floribunda' is a more compact and freely flowering plant, but it is less commonly available.

COMMON NAME
Yesterday, Today and Tomorrow Plant

Plant type	Flowering plant with erect, bushy habit
Season of interest	Spring and summer, occasionally all year round
Size	30–60cm (12–24in)
Flower	4–5cm (1½–2in), purple fading to pale blue then off-white, fragrant
Leaf	Oval, green, shiny 7.5–10cm (3–4in)
Temperature	16–20°C (61–68°F)
Aspect/Light	Well-lit situation, with some exposure to sun
Humidity	Moderate to high
Watering	Evenly moisten compost in spring and summer, allowing to dry out a little before re-watering; water just enough to prevent drying out in autumn and winter
Feeding	Once every three to four weeks with flowering plant fertilizer in spring and summer
Propagation	Plant 10cm (4in) tip cuttings or semi-hardwood cuttings in seed and cutting compost at 20–21°C (68–70°F) in spring
Potting	Houseplant potting compost
Problems	Red spider mite
Availability	Occasionally available
Uses	Grow in container on its own or in group
Other varieties	B.p.c. 'Floribunda' – more compact and freely flowering B.p.c. 'Macrantha' – larger flowers, up to 5–7.5cm (2–3in) across

Regularly pinch out the growing tips to promote compact growth

Calceolaria integrifolia 'Sunshine'

A spectacular, small tender perennial, normally grown as an annual, which is ideal for container planting and makes a showy pot plant in the cool conservatory. The Calceolaria is fairly easy to raise from seed and it should be massed in small or large groups for best effect. Its bright golden-yellow colour and long flowering period make it invaluable in a mixed display of flowering plants. For the best results, feed and water well throughout the growing period and make sure the plant receives plenty of direct sunlight. The range of colours in the varieties includes white, yellow, orange and red.

COMMON NAME
Slipperwort

Plant type	Flowering plant with bushy habit
Season of interest	Early summer to autumn
Size	25cm (12in) high
Flower	Bladder-like, 1.25cm ($\frac{1}{2}$in) across, borne in loose clusters, bright yellow
Leaf	Oval, 4–5cm ($1\frac{1}{2}$–2in) long, soft-textured and downy, grey-green
Temperature	0–5°C (32–41°)
Aspect/light	Sunny position
Humidity	Moderate
Watering	Water well throughout the summer growing period
Feeding	Flowering plant fertilizer every two weeks during the summer growing period
Propagation	sow seeds in seed and cutting compost at 18°C (64°F) in March/April
Potting	Houseplant potting compost
Problems	Whitefly
Availability	Commonly available in late spring to early summer
Uses	Grow in pot or container; can be used on its own or in groups

Callistemon hybrids

Fluffy cylindrical flower spikes give this unusual Australian shrub its popular name of Bottle Brush. The variety most commonly seen is *C. citrinus* with deep red flower spikes, but yellow, white and even green flowers are also available.

The plant flowers in summer. Like most Australian shrubs, Callistemons need plenty of light, and pot-grown plants can be placed outside in summer. They can become straggly if left unpruned, and should be cut back in the autumn. However, before pruning too hard, bear in mind that the following year's flowers will appear on new growth made after flowering.

COMMON NAME
Bottle Brush

Plant type	Flowering shrub with upright habit
Season of interest	Summer to early autumn
Size	To 90cm (36in)
Flower	Cylindrical 'brush' made up of stamens, 7.5–10cm (3–4in) long, red, white, yellow, green, produced in summer to early autumn
Leaf	Narrow, evergreen, 7.5cm (3in) long
Temperature	−3–20°C (26–68°F)
Aspect/Light	Well-lit situation with exposure to sunlight
Humidity	Moderate to dry
Watering	Water well from spring to autumn; keep on drier side in winter
Feeding	Once every four weeks with flowering plant fertilizer in spring and early summer
Propagation	Plant 7.5–10cm (3–4in) stem cuttings in seed and cutting compost or low-lime compost at 15–18°C (59–6°F) in spring; sow seeds in seed and cutting compost at 13–18°C (55–65°F) in spring
Potting	Lime-free or ericaceous compost
Problems	May become open in habit
Availability	Quite commonly available throughout the year
Uses	Grow in container or conservatory bed; normally grown on its own; can be moved outside in summer

To cut down on water loss, plunge the roots into a peat substitute, gravel or soil

Camellia hybrids

Camellias are usually thought of as hardy plants but they are also ideal for growing in the conservatory. Their spectacular flowers make a welcome splash of colour in early spring. The glossy, dark, evergreen foliage makes a striking contrast to the beautiful single or double red, pink or white blooms. Camellias can be temperamental if they are not provided with the right conditions. They must be grown in lime-free or ericaceous compost, dislike sudden changes in temperature or moisture levels, and will not flourish in a hot, dry atmosphere. If possible, they should be watered with lime-free water or with rainwater. They require only light pruning in early spring to remove untidy shoots.

COMMON NAME
Camellia

Plant type	Flowering shrub with upright habit
Season of interest	Spring
Size	To 180 cm (72in)
Flower	Single or double, 7.5–12.5cm (3–5in), white, and shades of red and pink or bi-coloured
Leaf	Oval, 10cm (4in), dark green, glossy, evergreen
Temperature	−3–18°C (26–65°F)
Aspect/Light	Well-lit situation out of direct sun
Humidity	Moderate
Watering	Evenly moisten compost throughout the year; do not use water containing lime
Feeding	Once every two to three weeks with flowering plant fertilizer in late spring and early summer
Potting	Peat-based ericaceous potting compost
Propagation	Plant 10cm (3in) tip cuttings in low-lime compost at 13–16°C (55–61°F) in late summer
Problems	Dehydration in warm, dry atmosphere
Availability	Commonly available throughout the year
Uses	Grow in container or conservatory bed; usually grown on its own

Pinch out the leading shoots in spring to encourage a bushy habit

Campsis tagliabuana 'Mme Gallen'

A spectacular flowering climber from China and Eastern Asia, suitable for a large conservatory or greenhouse. Its panicles of orange-red, trumpet-shaped flowers provide a brilliant splash of colour in late summer and early autumn. Orange and yellow-flowered varieties are also available. Although it is slow to establish itself, the Campsis will eventually cover an area of up to 10 x 10m (33 x 33ft) and should be trained on wires or a trellis. Unwanted shoots should be cut back after the leaves fall in autumn. Plenty of sunshine is needed if the plant is to flower well.

COMMON NAMES
Trumpet Climber or Creeper

Plant type	Flowering plant with climbing habit
Season of interest	Late summer to autumn
Size	To 10 x 10m (33 x 33ft)
Flower	In panicles of 6–12, Trumpet-shaped, to 7.5cm (3in) long, orange, orange-red or yellow
Leaf	Pinnate, 7–9 oval, toothed leaflets up to 7.5 cm (3in) long, light green, on twining stems
Temperature	Minimum − 10°C (14°F) in winter
Aspect/Light	Well-lit situation with plenty of sunshine
Humidity	Moderate
Watering	As required
Feeding	In early summer with flowering plant liquid fertilizer
Propagation	Plant 7.5–10cm (3–4in) tip cuttings in seed and cutting compost at 16–21°C (61–70°F) in summer
Potting	For best results grow in open soil
Problems	May be slow to flower after planting
Availability	Commonly available throughout the year
Uses	Grow in conservatory bed and train on wires or trellis
Other varieties	C. *tagliabuana* – orange flowers; C. *t.* 'Yellow Trumpet' – yellow flowers

To train the growth horizontally, tie the plant to wires supported with vine eyes

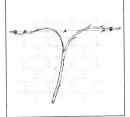

Canna indica hybrids

This handsome perennial, from the tropics of South America, has large, oval, green or purple leaves, which show off to good effect the large columns of red, orange or yellow flowers. The combination of foliage and flower colour depends on the variety. The Canna is often used in the garden as a summer bedding plant. Given the protection of a conservatory, though, it can be grown for many years. Plants are normally propagated by removing short sections of the fleshy underground stems, which readily take root and send up strong leaves and flowering shoots in spring, to flower in summer.

COMMON NAME
Indian Shot

Propagate the plant from root cuttings in mid spring

Plant type	Flowering and foliage plant with erect habit
Season of interest	All year round, especially summer and autumn
Size	100–120cm (39–48in) in height, 30–60cm (12–24in) in spread
Flower	In spikes, orange, red or yellow
Leaf	Oval to lance-shaped, 40cm (15in) or more long, 12cm (5in) wide, blue or purple
Temperature	5–77°C (41–77°F)
Aspect/Light	Full sun to light shade
Humidity	Average
Watering	Evenly moisten compost in spring and summer; reduce in autumn; water rarely in winter
Feeding	Liquid houseplant fertilizer after flowering
Propagation	Root 8cm (3in) sections of underground stem in houseplant potting compost in mid spring
Potting	Houseplant potting compost
Problems	Root-rot from over-watering
Availability	Quite commonly available as sections of underground stem in mid spring; occasionally available as plants
Uses	Grow in container

Capsicum annuum

Colourful, edible fruits are the main feature of the Capsicum or Red Sweet Pepper. These are usually produced in shades of yellow, orange and red, though there are also purple varieties. The fleshy, cone-shaped or pointed fruits remain decorative for up to twelve weeks before becoming wrinkled and falling from the plant. The fruits are preceded by small white flowers in summer or autumn. The plant needs plenty of light for best results, and the compost must not be allowed to dry out otherwise both the leaves and the fruit may fall prematurely. Regular mist spraying of the leaves will also be appreciated by the plant. The Capiscum is usually grown from seed, but is not easy to propagate.

COMMON NAME
Red Sweet Pepper

Plant type	Fruiting plant with shrubby habit
Season of interest	Autumn to winter
Size	30–45cm (12–18in)
Flower	White, insignificant
Leaf	Oval, 5–10cm (2–4in), green
Temperature	13–21°C (55–65°F)
Aspect/Light	Well-lit situation with some direct sun
Humidity	Moderate
Watering	Keep compost evenly moist and do not allow to dry out
Feeding	Once every two weeks with houseplant fertilizer in spring and summer
Propagation	Sow seeds in seed and cutting compost at 21–24°C (70–75°F) in early spring; difficult
Potting	Houseplant potting compost
Problems	Leaves and fruit may drop if compost is allowed to dry out
Availability	Commonly available from autumn to early winter
Uses	Grow in container and display either on its own or in groups

Spray the plant with water in summer and autumn to help pollinate the flowers

A striking plant with broad, deeply veined leaves and strange crested flower heads in shades of red and yellow. Celosias are sometimes grown in the garden as summer bedding plants, but they are also ideal for display in pots or containers in the conservatory, where they may remain in flower for several weeks. The flowering period is from mid to late summer. For best results, Celosias need a coolish, well-ventilated position with some direct sunlight, and they should be fed regularly to prolong the flowering period. When flowering has finished, the plants are usually discarded.

COMMON NAME
Cockscomb

Group odd numbers of pots together to produce a bold display

Plant type	Flowering plant with upright habit
Season of interest	Summer
Size	30–60cm (12–24in)
Flower	Crested plume, 7.5–15cm (3–6in), red and yellow
Leaf	Broad, lance-like, 10cm (4in), deeply veined
Temperature	10–16°C (50–61°F)
Aspect/light	Well-lit situation with some sunlight
Humidity	Moderate
Feeding	Every two weeks with flowering plant; fertilizer in spring and summer
Propagation	Sow seed in seed and cutting compost at 18°C (64°F) in early spring
Problems	Can look untidy towards end of flowering period
Availability	Quite commonly available throughout the year
Uses	Grow in pot or container and use on its own or as part of mixed display
Other varieties	*C. plumosa* – plume-like flower heads, coloured yellow, red, pink and orange

Cestrum hybrids

Cestrums are evergreen or semi-evergreen shrubs with attractive clusters of tubular flowers similar to those of the Jasmine.

They can grow quite tall and may be vigorous, so are best suited to the conservatory. The ideal growing position is near a wall or pillar. There are several types of Cestrum, most of which are sweetly scented. *C. nocturnum* and *C. parqui* are both night-flowering with strongly scented white flowers. *C. elegans* has red flowers and purple berries. *C. e.* 'Smith' has pinkish flowers. *C. auranticum* has orange flowers. All of these are day-flowering. Cestrums should be pruned back hard in late winter.

COMMON NAME
Hammer bush

Plant type	Flowering plant with spreading habit
Season of interest	Early summer to early autumn
Size	150cm (60in) when grown in a pot, if not double
Flower	tubular, 2.5cm (1in) long, borne in clusters, red, deep pink, orange or white
Leaf	Oval, 5–7.5 cm (2–3in), green or greyish green
Temperature	−3–16°C (26–61°F)
Aspect/Light	Well-lit situation, shaded from bright sunlight
Humidity	Moderate
Watering	Evenly moisten compost in spring and autumn; keep on the drier side in autumn and winter with just enough moisture to prevent drying
Feeding	Every two to three weeks with flowering plant fertilizer in spring and early summer
Propagation	Plant 7.5–10cm (3–4in) stem cuttings in seed and cutting compost at 18–20°C (65–68°F) in spring
Potting	Peat-based ericaceous potting compost
Problems	Whitefly
Availability	Quite commonly available all year
Uses	Grow in container or conservatory bed, near wall or pillar

Plant the Cestrum at least 38–46cm (15–18in) away from the wall

Clematis, large-flowered hybrids

These beautiful climbers come in a wide range of forms and colours. Clematis need a soil containing plenty of organic material, and though their heads like to be in sun, their roots should be shaded. As well as climbing up walls, trellises, and pillars, they can be used as ground cover over a low wire frame. There are several different ways of pruning Clematis, depending on variety and time of flowering. For varieties intended to flower early, the best method is to tidy and thin end shoots back to the main framework after flowering. There are many large-flowered hybrids suitable for the cool conservatory.

COMMON NAME
Clematis

Train the plant up wires, 30cm (12in) apart, and held 5cm (2in) away from the wall with vine eyes

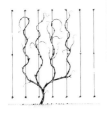

Plant type	Flowering plant with climbing habit
Season of interest	Mid spring to autumn
Size	To 210 × 210m (84 × 84in)
Flower	Flat, plate-shaped, 7.5–20cm (3–8in) wide, made up of 4–8 oval sepals; white, pink, red, mauve, purple, blue, single and double varieties; some varieties have coloured bar down centre of sepal
Leaf	Made up of 3–5 lance-like or oval leaflets, each up to 10cm (4in), mid-green, on twining leaf-stalks
Temperature	Minimum −5°C (23°F)
Aspect/Light	Full sun to light shade; roots must be shaded
Humidity	Moderate
Watering	Evenly moisten compost from spring to autumn, allowing to dry out a little before re-watering; keep on drier side in winter
Feeding	Every three weeks with flowering plant liquid fertilizer from mid spring to mid summer
Propagation	Plant 5cm (2in) internodal stem cuttings (2in) in sand and peat mix at 15–18°C (59–64°F) in summer
Potting	Soil-based potting compost
Problems	Clematis wilt and mildew, blackfly
Availability	Commonly available all year round
Uses	Grow in very large container or bed in cool conservatory; train up wires

Clematis, small-flowered hybrids

All of the small-flowered Clematis grow well in the conservatory, where their flowers can be shown to good effect. Their foliage is delicate and can form a valuable shade canopy. Most varieties require pruning. Those that flower in spring should be pruned after flowering; those that flower in the autumn should be cut back hard in spring. An attractive way to display these plants is to fan-train them up the conservatory wall. Varieties include *C. flammula*, with white flowers, *C. texensis*, with red flowers, *C. viticella*, with purple-red flowers, *C. macropetala*, with blue flowers and *C. alpina*, with violet flowers.

COMMON NAME
Small-flowered Clematis

Plant type	Flowering plant with climbing habit
Season of interest	Spring, summer or autumn, depending on variety
Size	4–5m (13–16ft) in height and spread
Flower	Either monk's-capped or star-like in shape, wide range of colours
Leaf	Up to 8cm (3in) long and wide, often heavily lobed
Temperature	−10–20°C (14–68°F)
Aspect/Light	Prefers full sun but will tolerate light shade
Humidity	Average
Watering	Evenly moisten compost in spring and summer; keep on dry side in autumn and winter
Feeding	Liquid houseplant fertilizer in spring and early summer
Propagation	Root semi-ripe cuttings in grit sand at 21°C (70°F)
Potting	Soil-based potting compost
Problems	Aphid
Availability	Commonly available from spring to summer
Uses	Grow in bed in cool conservatory; train up wires

Train the plant in a fan-shape up a trellis

Clerodendrum thomsoniae

An extraordinarily attractive plant that provides a long period of display, almost all through the growing season. To grow at its best, the plant needs not only a relatively high level of light, but also high humidity. With the right conditions it will grow quite vigorously and will need to be trained and kept in check. As a climbing plant, the Clerodendron will climb well up a cane frame or a trellis, with additional support from ties. After flowering, the plant can be trimmed or pruned to improve the overall shape and appearance. Another method of display is to grow the plant in a large hanging basket, where it will both trail loosely over the sides and climb up the support chains.

COMMON NAMES
Bleeding Heart Vine,
Glory Bower

The Clerodendrum can climb and trail effectively

Plant type	Flowering plant with climbing habit that can also trail
Season of interest	Late spring to early autumn
Size	150–250cm (59–98in)
Flower	Star-shaped, red flowers appearing from 2.5cm (1in) white calyx, produced in clusters
Leaf	Oval, almost heart-shaped, 7.5–10cm (3–4in), dark green
Temperature	15–21°C (59–70°F)
Aspect/Light	Well-lit position with some shade to filter direct sunlight
Humidity	High
Watering	Evenly moisten compost in spring and summer; keep on drier side in autumn and winter
Feeding	Once every two to three weeks with flowering plant fertilizer in spring and summer
Propagation	10–15cm (4–6in) cuttings in seed and cutting compost at 21–22°C (70–72°F) from late spring to early summer
Potting	Houseplant potting compost
Problems	Red spider mite
Availability	Not commonly available, but may be seen late in spring and summer, normally as small, bushy plant
Uses	Grow as climber in container or conservatory bed, with support; or use as climber and trailer in hanging basket

Clianthus puniceus

This uncommon climber comes from Australia and New Zealand. Its curiously shaped curved red flowers have given it the common name of Parrot Beak or Parrot Bill. The Clianthus can be used as a houseplant, but is more suited to the conservatory. The large and colourful flowers appear in spring. There is also a white form, *C. p.* 'Albus'. The Clianthus is fairly easy to grow in spite of its exotic appearance but needs good drainage and plenty of light for the best results. It is prone to red spider mite, so leaves should be mist sprayed regularly in summer. It can be propagated either from seed or cuttings.

COMMON NAMES
Parrot's Beak, Parrot Bill

Plant type	Flowering plant with climbing habit
Season of interest	Late spring to early summer
Size	180cm (72in) when grown in a pot, if not double
Flower	Unusual beak-like flowers, 7.5cm (2in) long, bright red or white
Leaf	Pinnate, green, 15cm (6in) long
Temperature	−2–20°C (28–68°F)
Aspect/Light	Very well-lit situation with shade only from brightest summer sun
Humidity	Moderate
Watering	Evenly moisten compost from spring to autumn; keep a little drier in winter
Feeding	Every two to three weeks with flowering plant fertilizer in spring and early summer
Propagation	Plant 7.5–10cm (3–4in) stem cuttings in seed and cutting compost at 16–18°C (61–64°F) in summer; sow seeds in seed and cutting compost at 13–16°C (55–61°F) in spring
Problems	Red spider mite
Availability	Quite commonly available throughout the year
Uses	Grow in large container or conservatory bed; can be fan-trained on wall

Water the Clianthus with rainwater if possible to avoid adding lime

Convolvulus mauritanicus

This creeping relative of the Common Bindweed is one of the most attractive plants in its family, and fortunately it does not have the invasive nature of the garden weed. The long, silver-grey shoots, carrying the silver-grey foliage, provide an elegant background to the pale blue, trumpet-shaped flowers. The Convolvulus is ideal for the conservatory, where it can either be trailed from a hanging pot or basket or used to provide carpet cover in a large tub or conservatory bed. The creeping habit of growth makes this shrub a very useful subject for an associated planting with larger flowering or foliage plants.

COMMON NAME
Blue Convolvulus

Create an attractive feature by growing the Convolvulus in an old chimney pot

Plant type	Flowering shrub with creeping habit
Season of interest	Mid spring to late summer
Size	Up to 100cm (39in) spread
Flower	Open-ended trumpet, pale blue
Leaf	Oval, 5cm (2in) long, grey to blue-grey
Temperature	$-2-20°C$ (27–68°F)
Aspect/Light	Full sun; dislikes shade
Humidity	Moderate
Watering	Keep compost evenly moist from late spring to early autumn; keep on dry side in winter
Feeding	Liquid fertilizer in mid spring
Propagation	Sow seed at 18–20°C (64–68°F); root semi-ripe cuttings in grit sand in mid summer
Potting	Houseplant potting compost
Problems	Red spider mite, vine weevil
Availability	Quite commonly available as a bedding plant or houseplant, particularly in spring and summer
Uses	Grow in container either on its own or in mixed group

Cytisus × racemosus

This hybrid cross between the Canary Islands and Madagascan Broom is an elegant, arching shrub, which often exceeds 120cm (48in) in height and spread. The three-fingered, grey, hairy leaves and grey-green stems provide a perfect foil for the racemes of bright yellow flowers, which are produced in late spring and also intermittently through the summer. With its Broom parentage, this plant is tolerant of hot, sunny, dry conditions, making it an ideal choice for the conservatory. It requires a fair amount of space to show off its graceful, arching habit to best effect.

COMMON NAME
Tender Broom

Plant type	Flowering shrub with arching habit
Season of interest	Spring to early summer
Size	100–200cm (36–72in) or more
Flower	Racemes, 5–10cm (2–4in) long, bright yellow
Leaf	Three-fingered, oval to round, up to 2cm (¾in) long, silky-hairy, grey-green, evergreen
Temperature	0–10°C (32–50°F)
Aspect/Light	Full sun; dislikes shade
Humidity	Average
Watering	Moisten compost sparingly in spring and summer; keep on dry side in autumn and winter
Feeding	Once every spring with liquid houseplant fertilizer
Propagation	Grown by grafting; best purchased as finished plant
Potting	Houseplant potting compost with 25 per cent grit sand added to aid drainage
Problems	Limited attacks of red spider mite, aphid
Availability	Quite commonly available from spring to summer
Uses	Grow in large container and display on its own; can be moved outside in summer

Add a surface layer of pebbles to the pot to keep the stem dry

Datura arborea

The spectacular white, trumpet-shaped flowers of the Datura make an exotic show in the conservatory, but should be handled with caution as all parts of the plant are poisonous. The flowers, which are very fragrant, appear from early summer to autumn. The Datura is a large shrub, up to 3m (10ft) tall. It should be pruned in early spring, cutting back the previous year's shoots to within 15cm (6in) of the base of the plant. A similar species, often confused with *D. arborea*, is *D.* x *candida*. This has even larger flowers, up to 30cm (12in) long, which are usually white, but may also be cream or pink.

COMMON NAME
Angel's Trumpet

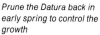

Prune the Datura back in early spring to control the growth

Plant type	Flowering plant with erect habit
Season of Interest	Summer to autumn
Size	3m (10ft)
Flower	Trumpet-shaped, 18–20cm (7–8in) long, white, fragrant
Leaf	Oval, pointed, 22.5cm (9in), mid-green, hairy
Temperature	10–20°C (5–68°F)
Aspect/Light	Well-lit situation with shade from summer sun
Humidity	Moderate
Watering	Keep compost evenly moist from spring to autumn; keep on drier side in winter
Feeding	Every three weeks with houseplant liquid fertilizer from mid spring to mid summer
Propagation	Plant 10–15cm (4–6in) tip cuttings in seed and cutting compost at 15–18°C (59–64°F) in late spring
Potting	Soil-based potting compost with 25 per cent extra organic material such as rotted leaf mould
Problems	Red spider mite
Availability	Limited availability throughout the year
Uses indoors	Indoor, conservatory or greenhouse plant for container or border
Uses	Grown in large container and display on its own; can be moved outside in summer

Euphorbia pulcherrima

A boldly coloured plant that is a popular feature at Christmas. The large bracts, which may be red, pink, or creamy white, remain attractive for three or four months. After this time the plant should be pruned hard back, by a half to two-thirds. It can then be left to grow as a foliage plant or an attempt can be made to encourage the bracts to grow again the following winter. This involves keeping the plant in complete darkness after the hours of daylight at the end of summer. To avoid leaf loss keep the plant at a constant temperature and avoid over-watering.

COMMON NAMES
Poinsettia, Flower of the Holy Night, Christmas Plant

Plant type	Flowering plant with upright, bushy habit
Season of interest	Winter and early spring
Size	20–100cm (8–39in)
Flower	Tiny, petal-less yellow flowers produced amidst red, pink or cream-white bracts, 10–15cm (4–6in)
Leaf	Lobed, 7.5–12.5cm (3–5in) long, mid to dark green with pinkish red stems
Temperature	16–21°C (61–70°F)
Aspect/Light	Well lit position with very slight shade from brightest sun
Humidity	Moderate
Watering	Evenly moisten compost from spring to autumn, allowing to dry out a little before re-watering; keep drier in winter
Feeding	Once every two to three weeks with flowering plant fertilizer in spring and summer
Propagation	Plant 7.5cm (3in) tip cuttings in 6cm (2½in) diam. pot of seed and cutting compost at 21–22°C (70–72°F) from mid spring to early summer
Potting	Houseplant potting compost
Problems	White fly, leaf loss if over-watered or subjected to draughts or cold
Availability	Commonly available, especially around Christmas
Uses	Grow in large container; use for seasonal colour at Christmas and New Year

In mid spring cut the plant back by a half to two-thirds

Felicia amelloides

Pretty blue daisy-like flowers with yellow centres can be found on this dainty shrub for much of the year, though the summer is its main flowering season. These flowers will open fully only in sunshine, so this plant needs plenty of light and a sunny position. The leaves of the Felicia are green or variegated. For the best display, and to maintain a compact, bushy shape, growing tips should be pinched back regularly.

When doing this be careful to avoid pinching out the stems which carry the flower buds. Keep the compost moist at all times. The Felicia needs plenty of water and sunshine to flower well.

COMMON NAME
Blue Marguerite

Plant type	Flowering plant with bushy habit
Season of interest	All year round, especially summer
Size	30–60cm (12–24in)
Flower	Daisy-like, 2.5cm (1in) across, blue with yellow centre
Leaf	Oval, 2.5cm (1in), dark green or variegated
Temperature	0–3°C (32–37°F)
Aspect/Light	Well-lit situation with exposure to sunlight
Humidity	Moderate
Watering	Keep compost moist at all times
Feeding	Every three weeks with flowering plant liquid fertilizer from late spring to late summer
Propagation	Plant 7.5–10cm (3–4in) stem cuttings in seed and cutting compost at 4–10°C (40–50°F) in spring; sow seed in seed and cutting compost at 16°C (61°F) in summer.
Potting	Houseplant potting compost
Problems	None
Availability	Commonly available as a bedding plant in spring; at other times as a houseplant
Uses	Grow in container either on its own or in groups

Remove the lower leaves of cuttings then root them in sharp sand

Gardenia jasminoides

The rich, almost heady fragrance of the Gardenia must be one of the most distinctive perfumes in the world. The plant prefers to grow in an acid compost and should ideally be watered with rain water to avoid the problems caused by the calcium in tap water. The Gardenia can also suffer from chlorosis, a yellowing of the leaves caused by an iron deficiency. This can usually be corrected by watering with a solution of sequestrated iron (iron sequestrene), which will turn the leaves back to a healthy, deep green colour. To prevent the plant becoming leggy and untidy, it should be pruned lightly in early spring. Alternatively, a more drastic prune, by up to a half or even two thirds, may encourage the plant to grow back more in balance.

COMMON NAMES
Gardenia, Cape Jasmine

Plant type	Flowering plant with bushy habit
Season of interest	Summer
Size	15–45cm (6–18in)
Flower	5–7.5cm (2–3in) double, white, with rich, heavy fragrance
Leaf	Oval, 5cm (2in) long, glossy, dark green
Temperature	18–21°C (64–70°F)
Aspect/Light	Well-lit situation with shade from direct sun
Humidity	High
Watering	Evenly moisten compost in spring and summer, allowing to dry a little before re-watering; keep on drier side in autumn and winter
Feeding	Once every two to three weeks with flowering plant fertilizer in spring and summer
Propagation	Plant 7.5–10cm (3–4in) tip cuttings in seed and cutting compost at 15–20°C (60–68°F) from mid to late spring or early autumn
Potting	Ericaceous compost
Problems	Aphid, mealy bug, scale insect, red spider mite, chlorosis
Availability	Often available in spring and summer
Uses	Grow in clay pot or container either on its own or in groups

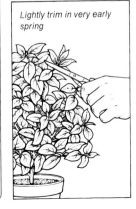

Lightly trim in very early spring

Gerbera jamesonii

The Gerbera, a native plant of South Africa, is a popular variety with cut flower arrangers as well as with conservatory gardeners. It has attractive single or double daisy-like flowers in a range of vivid colours, including pink, red, orange, yellow and white; all varieties have yellow centres to the flowers. The flower stalks can be up to 60cm (24in) long and the height of the plant makes it especially suitable for a mixed flowering display in the conservatory. The Gerbera likes a brightly-lit position with some sunshine. It should not be over-watered, and requires good drainage. This plant is a perennial, and can be propagated by division in spring as well as grown from seed.

COMMON NAME
Gerbera

Stand a few pots in an ornamental bowl to achieve a good display

Plant type	Flowering plant with upright habit
Season of interest	Spring; some imported plants at other times
Size	To 60cm (24in)
Flower	Daisy-like, 5cm (2in) across, single or double, red, pink, orange, yellow or white, with yellow centre
Leaf	Lobed, 15cm (6in), green
Temperature	10–21°C (50–70°F)
Aspect/Light	Well-lit situation with exposure to sunshine
Humidity	Moderate
Watering	Keep compost moist from spring to autumn, but do not over-water; keep on the dry side in winter
Feeding	Every two weeks with flowering plant fertilizer during the mid spring to early summer growing period
Propagation	Sow seed in seed and cutting compost at 18–21°C (65–70°F) in spring; divide established plants in spring
Potting	Houseplant potting compost
Problems	Greenfly, red spider mite
Availability	Moderate availability throughout the year
Uses	Grow in container and display on its own or in group

Gloriosa rothschildiana

The flowers of the Gloriosa are among the most spectacular of all plants. They are bright red and yellow in colour, and have an unusual lily-like shape. The long, glossy leaves bear tendrils at their tips, and the plant must be provided with a frame or trellis to climb up. All of the growth on the plant, which can be prodigious, is produced in one year's growing season. At the end of the season the plant dies back to its tuberous root, which should be kept fairly dry and cool, at 10–13°C (50–55°F), When spring arrives, the moisture and warmth can be increased to encourage the plant to break out of dormancy. The tuber does not always respond immediately so it is sometimes necessary to persevere for a while until the new growth begins.

COMMON NAME

Glory Lily

Plant type	Flowering plant with climbing habit
Season of interest	Summer
Size	100–200cm (39–78in)
Flower	Formed from six recurved petals, 7.5–10cm (3–4in) across, red and yellow
Leaf	Pointed, thin, 7.5cm (3in) long, shiny, dark green
Temperature	15–20°C (59–68°F)
Aspect/Light	Well-lit situation with exposure to sunlight
Humidity	High
Watering	Evenly moisten compost in spring and summer; keep on dry side in autumn and winter
Feeding	Once every two to three weeks with half-strength flowering plant fertilizer in spring and summer
Propagation	Separate tuber and pot in potting compost at 18–20°C (65–68°F) in very early spring; sow seeds as above in mid spring
Potting	Houseplant potting compost
Problems	Aphid, difficulty in breaking out of dormancy
Availability	Occasionally available
Uses	Grow in container or conservatory bed and train up frame, trellis or wires

A frame is useful for the plant to climb up

Hoya bella

This Hoya is one of the best plants for a hanging pot. The flowers are attractive when viewed from above or from the side, but they are most beautiful when viewed from below, as the rose-purple centres can be seen. Apart from being a good trailing plant, it can also climb weakly, with support from a small frame or trellis. It is a delicate subject and particular care should be taken to avoid over-watering, temperature fluctuations or physical disturbance, any of which can cause the developing flowers to be shed. A clay pot is perhaps the best container as it provides more stability and allows the roots to be aerated. To keep stress to a minimum, the plant should be repotted only when it becomes absolutely necessary.

COMMON NAME
Miniature Wax Plant

A clay pot will provide more stability

Plant type	Flowering plant with trailing, semi-climbing habit
Season of interest	Spring and summer, occasionally other times
Size	20–400cm (8–156in) either climbing or trailing
Flower	Pendulous, five-petalled, white with a rose-purple centre, fragrant, in clusters
Leaf	Pointed, spear-like, 2.5cm (1in), dark green, leathery
Temperature	15–21°C (59–70°F)
Aspect/Light	Reasonably well-lit situation
Humidity	Moderate to high
Watering	Evenly moisten compost in spring and summer, allowing to get on the dry side before re-watering; keep drier in autumn and winter; water with care at all times
Feeding	Once every three to four weeks with flowering plant fertilizer in spring and summer
Propagation	Plant 7.5–10cm (3–4in) tip or stem cuttings in seed and cutting compost at 18–20°C (65–68°F) from mid spring to late summer
Potting	Houseplant potting compost
Problems	Mealy bug, root loss if over-watered
Availability	Occasionally available in spring and summer
Uses	Grow in clay pot or bed and train up frame; or grow in hanging basket

Hoya carnosa

An attractive, freely flowering plant that is quite easy to grow, provided it is not over-watered. It is a particularly useful climbing plant, having long stems that rapidly entwine the support. As it can climb to quite a height it is best displayed at floor level. The variety *H.c.* 'Variegata' is a little less hardy and freely flowering, but it does have quite attractive foliage. Both types are particularly prone to infestation by the mealy bug, which can be difficult to control. The pest is very good at hiding amongst the entwined stems and foliage, and as the plant is quite 'stiff', it is not easy to treat by general spraying. It is therefore best to make regular checks and spray each bug as it is found.

COMMON NAMES
Wax Plant, Wax Flower

Plant type	Flowering plant with climbing habit
Season of interest	Summer
Size	100–250cm (39–98in)
Flower	Fragrant, white to pale pink with red centre, in clusters of ten to thirty
Leaf	Pointed oval, fleshy, 7.5cm (3in) long, green, leathery
Temperature	18–21°C (64–70°F)
Aspect/Light	Well-lit situation with exposure to sunlight
Humidity	Moderate
Watering	Evenly moisten compost in spring and summer, allowing to dry a little before re-watering; keep on drier side in autumn and winter, watering just enough to prevent drying out
Feeding	Once every three to four weeks with flowering plant fertilizer in spring and summer
Propagation	Plant 10–12.5cm (4–5in) tip or stem cuttings in seed and cutting compost at 20°C (68°F) in spring
Potting	Houseplant potting compost
Problems	Mealy bug, root loss if over-watered
Availability	Occasionally available in spring and summer
Uses	Grow in conservatory bed or large container and train up wall and along roof
Other varieties	*H.c.* 'Variegata' – variegated foliage; more shy to flower

The plant may be displayed on a frame

Ipomoea hederacea

Ipomoea hederacea, the Morning Glory, is one of the most striking of all the Convolvulus family. Normally grown as an annual climber outdoors, it is also suitable for displaying in the conservatory. Its twining habit of growth will enable it to scramble over wires or trellis, or through the branches of a shrub. This is an extremely fast-growing plant – grown in a conservatory bed it should reach a height and spread of 3.7 × 3.7m (12 × 12ft) within the first year. The Ipomoea needs a sunny position to do well, where its bright blue trumpet-shaped flowers will be produced freely from mid summer to autumn, opening each day with the morning sun and fading at night.

COMMON NAME
Morning Glory

Plant several Ipomoeas together to achieve a bold display

Plant type	Flowering plant with climbing habit
Season of interest	Mid summer to early autumn
Size	180 × 180cm (72 × 72in) when grown in a pot, if not double
Flower	Five-petalled, trumpet-shaped, 6cm (2½in) wide, bright blue with white eye
Leaf	Broad, heart-shaped, up to 12.5cm (5in) long
Temperature	10 – 20°C (50 – 68°F)
Aspect/Light	Full sun
Humidity	Moderate
Watering	Water well during growing period
Feeding	Every two weeks with flowering plant fertilizer during late spring to early summer
Propagation	Sow seed in seed and cutting compost at 18°C (64°F) in early spring
Potting	Houseplant or soil-based potting compost
Problems	Slugs and snails may damage leaves; young plants very susceptible to over-watering
Availability	Commonly available as a bedding plant from late spring to early summer or seed from early winter
Uses	Grow in conservatory bed and train up wires or trellis

Jasminum polyanthum

The Jasminum can be a very effective indoor plant provided it is grown in a cool, light and airy situation. When small it can be trained around a wire hoop or similar support, but will eventually need a larger cane frame. Near constant attention is necessary to keep control of the plant, as the growing shoots are extremely vigorous and can entwine around virtually anything that gets in the way. The common name of Pink Jasmine comes from the colour of the flower buds, which are pale pink before opening into the pure white, exquisitely scented flowers. If grown at a fairly cool temperature, the plant can remain in flower for many weeks, from the middle of winter to the middle of spring.

COMMON NAMES
Pink Jasmine, Indoor Jasmine, Jessamine

Plant type	Flowering plant with climbing habit
Season of interest	Mid winter to mid spring
Size	100–200cm (39–78in)
Flower	Five-petalled, 1.25cm ($\frac{1}{2}$in) across, white, scented, in clusters
Leaf	Five to seven leaflets produced in opposite pairs
Temperature	10–15°C (50–59°F)
Aspect/Light	Well-lit situation with some exposure to sunlight
Humidity	Moderate
Watering	Evenly moisten compost in spring and summer, allowing to dry very slightly between waterings; keep on drier side in autumn and winter
Feeding	Once every two to four weeks with flowering plant fertilizer in spring and summer
Propagation	Plant 10cm (4in) tip or stem cuttings in seed and cutting compost at 18–20°C (65–68°F) from late spring to early autumn
Potting	Houseplant potting compost
Problems	Aphid
Availability	Commonly available from mid winter to mid spring
Uses	Grow in large container or bed and train up wall and along ridge of roof

Regularly train the growing shoots to prevent them becoming tangled

Lagerstroemia indica

This attractive shrub, a native of China, may also be grown outdoors in some areas, but is not reliably hardy when exposed to temperatures below freezing. It makes an ideal subject for featuring in the conservatory, where its clusters of deep-pink or purple flowers should appear in profusion in late summer. There is also a white form, *L. i.* 'Alba'. The Crepe Myrtle grows up to 10m (30ft) when used outdoors, so plants grown in the conservatory need to be pruned back hard each winter to keep their size in check. This is a deciduous shrub and it may lose its leaves in autumn.

COMMON NAME
Crepe Myrtle

Remove old flower heads after flowering to encourage new flowers

Plant type	Flowering shrub with upright habit
Season of interest	Mid to late summer
Size	To 180cm (72in) when grown in a pot, if not double
Flower	White, pink or purple, 2–3in (5–7cm) wide, in panicles
Leaf	Oval, 4–7.5cm (1½–3in) long, on short stalks
Temperature	0–3°C (32–37°F)
Aspect/Light	Well-lit situation
Humidity	Moderate
Watering	Keep compost evenly moist, allowing to dry a little before re-watering
Feeding	Every three weeks with flowering plant liquid fertilizer from late spring to mid summer
Propagation	Root 7cm (3in) stem cuttings in sand and grit at 10–12°C (50–55°F) in early summer
Potting	Soil-based potting compost
Problems	Red spider mite, overall size
Availability	Limited throughout the year
Uses	Grow on its own in large container or conservatory bed; can be fan-trained on wall

Lantana alba

The individual florets which make up the Lantana's round, tightly-packed flower heads change colour as they age, so that each head contains several different shades of colour. Colours include yellows, oranges, pinks, reds, bicolours and white. The flowering season lasts from spring to late autumn, so this is a very desirable shrub for any conservatory. If left unpruned it will reach a height of about 120cm (48in), but it can be restricted to 30–60cm (12–24in) by cutting back in late winter. This shrub can also be grown as a standard. Lantanas need plenty of sunlight and good drainage in order to flower well.

COMMON NAME
Lantana

Plant type	Flowering shrub with upright habit
Season of interest	Mid-spring to late autumn
Size	30–120cm (12–48in)
Flower	Circular heads of tightly-packed florets, 5cm (2in) across, varying shades of yellow, orange, pink, red or white
Leaf	Oval, pointed, 5cm (2in) long, grey-green
Temperature	10–21°C (50–70°F)
Aspect/Light	Well-lit situation with plenty of sunshine
Humidity	Moderate
Watering	Evenly moisten compost from spring to autumn, allowing to dry a little before re-watering; keep on the drier side in winter
Feeding	Once every two weeks with flowering plant fertilizer from spring to autumn
Propagation	Plant 7.5cm (3in) tip cuttings in seed and cutting compost at 16–18°C (61–64°F) in late summer
Potting	Houseplant potting compost
Problems	Red spider mite
Availability	Quite commonly available throughout the year
Uses	Grow on its own in large container or conservatory bed

The Lantana can be grown as a standard plant

Lapageria rosea

Lapageria rosea, the Chilean Bellflower, is one of the most attractive climbing plants suitable for the conservatory. The distinctive, bell-shaped flowers are produced almost all year round and last extremely well. The best-known varieties of the plant are pink or white but there are now a number of hybrids available, including doubles and bicolours, in all shades from cream and pale pink to near-red. The Lapageria is a lime-hater, so must be grown in a lime-free or ericaceous compost. It requires plenty of shade in summer and the roots should never be allowed to dry out. Propagation is possible by layering as well as from seed and stem cuttings.

COMMON NAME
Chilean Bellflower

Grow the plant up a wall and along the underside of a roof using a support wire and vine eyes

Plant type	Flowering plant with climbing habit
Season of interest	All year round
Size	To 180cm (72in) if grown in a pot, if not, double
Flower	Bell-shaped, to 7.5cm (3in) long, white to deep pink, single or double
Leaf	Oval, 7.5–15cm (3–6in) long, dark green, shiny
Temperature	Minimum 0–5°C (32–41°F)
Aspect/Light	Well-lit situation, shaded from direct summer sun
Humidity	Moderate
Watering	Keep compost evenly moist, allowing to dry out a little before re-watering
Feeding	Every three weeks with houseplant liquid fertilizer from late spring to mid summer
Propagation	Plant 7.5cm (3in) stem cuttings in seed and potting compost at 15–18°C (60–65°F) in early summer; sow seed at the same temperature all year round; peg down new shoots in seed and cutting compost in early summer
Problems	Aphids, mealy bug
Availability	Quite commonly available throughout the year
Uses	Grow in conservatory bed or large container and train up wall and along ridge of roof

Lippia citrodora

The leaves and stems of this small deciduous shrub have a lovely lemon scent when crushed, and are the source of an aromatic oil. The Lippia prefers a warm situation with plenty of sun and is thus ideally suited to the conservatory. It can be grown either in a large container or in a conservatory bed. A neat and attractive-looking plant, it has grey-green leaves and panicles of pale-mauve flowers appearing in summer. It should be pruned in spring, when the growth produced in the previous season can be cut back by a half.

COMMON NAME
Lemon Verbena

Plant type	Flowering plant with bushy habit
Season of interest	Spring to autumn
Size	To 90cm (36in)
Flower	Small, pale mauve, borne in terminal panicles in summer
Leaf	Lanceolate, 8–10cm (3–4in) long, grey-green, with strong lemon scent
Temperature	Minimum −2°C (28°F) in winter
Aspect/Light	Full sun
Humidity	Moderate
Watering	Evenly moisten compost in spring and summer, allowing to dry a little before re-watering; keep on dry side in autumn and winter
Feeding	Every three weeks with flowering plant liquid fertilizer from mid spring to mid summer
Propagation	Plant 7.5cm (3in) stem cuttings in seed and cutting compost at 16–18°C (51–64°F) in mid summer
Potting	Houseplant or soil-based potting compost
Problems	None
Availability	Quite commonly available throughout the year
Uses	Grow in large container, such as tub, or conservatory bed

Cut and dry surplus branches in mid summer for potpourri

Medinilla magnifica

A spectacular flowering plant that truly lives up to its name. The hanging flowerheads, which are up to 30cm (12in) long, consist of panicles of large bracts, rosy-pink in colour, with central purple and yellow anthers and forward-arching filaments. The colourful flowerheads contrast well with the broad, dark green, shiny leaves, making the Medinilla a handsome addition to the conservatory. Flowering mainly in spring, the plant may also bloom at other times of the year, depending on its cultivation. Being a tropical species, it requires a fair amount of warmth and should be sprayed with water once or twice a day throughout the year to increase the humidity level. *M. m* 'Rubra' is a variety with deeper pink flowers.

Plant type	Flowering plant with upright habit
Season of interest	Spring
Size	80–100cm (18–39in)
Flower	In panicles, 30cm (12in) long, pink flowers with purple and yellow anthers
Leaf	Oval, up to 30cm (12in) long, dark green, evergreen
Temperature	20–24°C (68–75°F)
Aspect/Light	Moderately to reasonably bright situation; avoid strong sunlight, which will cause scorching
Humidity	High
Watering	Keep compost evenly moist in spring and summer; water less in autumn and winter
Feeding	Once every three to four weeks with liquid houseplant fertilizer from spring to summer
Propagation	Root softwood cuttings in sand in closed case at not less than 21°C (70°F)
Potting	Houseplant potting compost
Problems	Mealy bug, root mealy bug, vine weevil; lack of humidity will lead to poor health
Availability	Quite commonly availble in spring
Uses	Grow in container either on its own or as part of group

Use a wire coat hanger bent into a 'Y' shape to support the flower heads

Myrtus communis

This highly attractive Mediterranean shrub makes an ideal plant for the conservatory. It is valuable for its scented leaves as well as for the flowers which appear throughout the summer, to be followed by purple berries in autumn. The variety most commonly grown indoors is *M. c. microphylla*, the Dwarf Myrtle. Myrtles can be pruned to the required shape by trimming the young shoots in spring. However, too-vigorous pruning will reduce the flowering potential. These plants require a lime-free soil and plenty of light. Pot-grown specimens can be put outside in summer if desired.

COMMON NAME
Myrtle

Plant type	Flowering plant with shrubby habit
Season of interest	Early summer to autumn
Size	60–180cm (24–72in)
Flower	White with prominent gold stamens, scented, 2cm (¾in) across
Leaf	Oval, 5cm (2in) long, dark green or variegated, aromatic
Temperature	0–3°C (32–37°F)
Aspect/Light	Well-lit situation with protection from bright summer sun
Humidity	Low to moderate
Watering	Water regularly from spring to autumn, allowing top layer of compost to dry out between waterings; keep on the dry side in winter
Feeding	Once very two weeks with flowering plant fertilizer in spring and early summer
Propagation	Plant 7.5–10cm (3–4in) stem cuttings in seed and cutting compost at 16°C (61°F) in summer
Potting	Lime-free or ericaceous compost
Problems	None
Availability	Quite commonly available throughout the year
Uses	Grow on its own in container

Myrtles can be clipped into a ball shape

Nerium oleander hybrids

An attractive, colourful plant that flowers freely throughout the summer. The large, occasionally fragrant blooms are borne in clusters above the lance-like leaves. Several varieties are available, producing pink, white or rose-red flowers. The disadvantage of the Nerium is that all parts of the plant are extremely poisonous, so it should be positioned well out of the reach of children. Provided this safety requirement can be met, it makes an ideal subject for the conservatory. In the summer, the plant will benefit from a spell outdoors. The Nerium is easy to propagate, from tip cuttings, although it is advisable to wear protective gloves when doing so or otherwise tending to the plant.

COMMON NAMES
Common Oleander, Rose Bay

Treat the plant with great care as all parts of it are poisonous

Plant type	Flowering plant with erect habit
Season of interest	Summer
Size	30–150cm (12–59in)
Flower	2.5cm (1in) across, pink, occasionally white or rose-red, in clusters of six to eight
Leaf	Lance-like, 10–15cm (4–6in) long, dark green
Temperature	15–21°C (59–70°F)
Aspect/Light	Full sun
Humidity	Moderate
Watering	Evenly moisten compost in spring and summer, allowing to dry a little before re-watering; keep on drier side in autumn and winter
Feeding	Once every two to three weeks with flowering plant fertilizer in spring and summer
Propagation	Plant 7.5–15cm (3–6in) tip cuttings in seed and cutting compost, or place in water, at 20–21°C (68–70°F) in early summer
Potting	Houseplant potting compost
Problems	Scale insect, mealy bug, aphid
Availability	Occasionally available from late spring to early summer
Uses	Grow on its own in container or conservatory bed

Passiflora caerulea

Provided cultural conditions are suitable, the Passiflora will produce its unusual and beautiful flowers in near continuous succession from summer to early autumn. With luck, these may be followed by the yellow to orange fruits. This plant is tidy and compact when young, but soon produces long, straggly growth with tendrils that latch on to almost anything nearby. It must therefore be carefully and regularly trained around an adequate supporting frame. If space is limited, the growth can be cut back hard each spring to keep the plant to a more manageable size. The Passiflora is a hardy subject, requiring cool conditions. In summer, container-grown plants can be stood outside if desired.

COMMON NAME
Passion Flower

Plant type	Flowering plant with climbing habit
Season of interest	Summer to early autumn
Size	60 – 250cm (24 – 98in)
Flower	7.5cm (3in) across, formed of five white sepals and five white petals with purple blue filaments radiating from centre, and with five yellow anthers and three brown stigmas, occasionally followed by 5cm (2in) yellow to orange fruit
Leaf	Lance-like, lobed, 7.5 – 10cm (3 – 4in), dark green, in clusters of five to nine
Temperature	16 – 21°C (61 – 70°F)
Aspect/Light	Well-lit position with sunlight
Humidity	Moderate to high
Watering	Evenly moisten compost in spring and summer, allowing to dry a little before re-watering; keep on dry side in autumn and winter
Feeding	Once every two to three weeks with flowering plant fertilizer in spring and summer
Propagation	Plant 10cm (4in) tip or stem cuttings in seed and cutting compost at 18 – 20°C (65 – 68°F) in early to mid summer
Potting	Houseplant potting compost
Problems	Aphid
Availability	Occasionally available in spring and early summer
Uses	Grow in container or large bed and train up wall or on wire ring or canes

Provide the plant with an adequate frame for support

Pelargonium domesticum

Pelargoniums are among the most popular flowering plants. Not only are they easy to grow, being quite hardy and tolerant of a certain amount of neglect, but they offer a long and rewarding flowering period. Preferring cool, well-lit positions, they are ideal plants for the conservatory. There are a number of varieties and cultivars available. *P. domesticum* has attractively patterned flowers, produced from late spring to early autumn, and pretty, scalloped leaves. It is, however, prone to attack by whitefly. *P. hortorum*, the Zonal Pelargonium, often called the Geranium, is the most common variety. It produces vibrantly coloured flowers nearly all year round, and is relatively free from problems. *P. peltatum* is a trailing variety with ivy-shaped leaves. It is a good plant for hanging pots and planters.

COMMON NAME
Regal Pelargonium

Remove faded flowers regularly

Plant type	Flowering plant with bushy habit
Season of interest	Late spring to early autumn
Size	15–60cm (6–24in)
Flower	Five-petalled, 5cm (2in), white, pink, lilac or red, clustered on 15–20cm (6–8in) stems
Leaf	Rounded heart-shaped with slightly serrated edge, 5–7.5cm (2–3in)
Temperature	16–20°C (61–68°F)
Aspect/Light	Well-lit position with sunlight
Humidity	Moderate
Watering	Evenly moisten compost in spring and summer, allowing to dry a little before re-watering; keep on drier side in autumn and winter, with just enough to prevent drying out
Feeding	Once every two to three weeks with flowering plant fertilizer in spring and summer
Propagation	Plant 10cm (4in) tip cuttings in seed and cutting compost at 18–20°C (65–68°F) from early to late summer
Potting	Houseplant potting compost
Problems	Whitefly, botrytis on fading flowers and leaves in cool, damp conditions
Availability	Commonly available spring and summer
Uses	Grow in container or conservatory bed as part of mixed planting
Other varieties	*P. hortorum* – 'zoned' leaf *P. peltatum* – ivy-shaped leaf

Pittosporum tobira

Pittosporums are Australian or New Zealand shrubs grown for their rosettes of shiny, dark green or variegated oval leaves; for their scented flowers in summer; and for the fruits which follow the flowers. *P. tobira* is not frost-hardy, so it is ideal for the conservatory. The tubular flowers are white or cream, borne in clusters. Their orange-blossom scent gives the plant its common-name of Mock Orange. The Pittosporum needs plenty of light to flower well, but it should be moved to a cool position for a rest in winter months. The variegated fir *P. t. variegatum* has added foliage attraction.

COMMON NAME
Mock Orange

Plant type	Flowering plant with shrubby habit
Season of interest	Flowers in summer; foliage all year round
Size	120–150cm (48–60in)
Flower	Tubular, scented, 1.25cm ($\frac{1}{2}$in) across, white or cream, followed by fruits
Leaf	Oval, shiny, dark green or variegated, 10cm (4in) long, borne in rosettes
Temperature	4.5–18°C (40–65°F); rest at 10°C (50°F) in winter
Aspect/Light	Well-lit situation with protection from direct summer sun
Humidity	Moderate
Watering	Water regularly in spring and summer, allowing top layer of compost to dry out between waterings; keep on dry side in autumn and winter
Feeding	Once every two weeks with flowering plant fertilizer in spring and early summer
Propagation	Plant 7.5cm (3in) tip cuttings in seed and cutting compost at 16–18°C (61–64°F) in spring
Problems	None
Availability	Limited availability throughout the year; often found in florists
Uses	Grow on its own in container or bed in cooler conservatory

Use the Pittosporum as a background to pot-grown bedding plants

Plumbago capensis

The sky-blue flowers of this lovely South African shrub make it a must for every conservatory. Produced in quantity in late summer and autumn, the tubular blossoms make a wonderful show at a time of year when flowering plants are becoming scarce. The flowers are produced on growth made the same year, so the old growths should be cut back by about two-thirds in early spring to encourage the plant to shoot vigorously during the growing season. The Plumbago makes a particularly attractive feature if the stems are trained up the conservatory wall in a fan-shape. As well as the blue Plumbago, there is a white form, *P. c.* 'Alba', but this is less spectacular.

COMMON NAME
Leadwort

Cut back old flowering shoots 2in (5cm) from the stem in early spring

Plant type	Flowering plant with leggy, upright habit
Season of interest	Late summer to autumn
Size	90–120cm (36–48in) when grown in a pot, if not double
Flower	Tubular with star-shaped face, 2.5cm (1in) across, clear blue or white
Leaf	Oval, mid-green, 5cm (2in) long
Temperature	7–20°C (45–68°F)
Aspect/Light	Well-lit situation with some sun
Humidity	Moderate
Watering	Keep compost evenly moist throughout growing period; keep on dry side in winter
Feeding	Once every two weeks with flowering plant fertilizer in spring and early summer
Propagation	Plant 7.5–10cm (3–4in) stem cuttings in seed and cutting compost at 21°C (70°F) in late summer; sow seed in seed and cutting compost at 21–24°C (70–75°F) in spring
Potting	Soil-based potting compost
Problems	Weak leggy habit of growth; overall size once established
Availability	Commonly available from late spring to early winter; limited availability at other times
Uses	Grow on its own in container or conservatory bed; can be fan-trained on wall

Prunus persica

Peaches and Nectarines may be grown in the conservatory with much success. They are best trained as fans against a wall, and should be planted in a border rather than pot-grown. They must be pruned hard after planting, taking the vertical central shoot down to the level of the first horizontal branches. The side branches are then tied in on wires. Regular pruning is needed in late winter, when shoots which have borne fruit must be cut back to new shoots. Flowering is in early spring when few insects are about, so flowers must be hand-pollinated to ensure a good crop of fruit in the autumn.

COMMON NAMES
Peach, Nectarine

Plant type	Flowering and fruiting tree with upright habit
Season of interest	Early spring to autumn
Size	To 4.6m (15ft)
Flower	Single, 2.5–4cm (1–1½in) across, pink; followed by round, fleshy, fuzzy or smooth skinned fruit, yellow flushed with red
Leaf	Lance-shaped, 5–10cm (2–4in), mid-green
Temperature	−5–16°C (23–61°F)
Aspect/Light	Well-lit situation with some direct sunlight
Humidity	Moderate
Watering	As required in spring and summer; drier in winter
Feeding	Every three weeks with liquid houseplant fertilizer from mid spring to midsummer
Propagation	Difficult to propagate young trees; best purchased from garden centre or nursery
Potting	Soil-based potting compost
Problems	Peach-leaf curl, red spider mite
Availability	Quite commonly available throughout the year
Uses	Grow on its own in bed in cooler conservatory; can be fan-trained on wall

Brush the flowers with a rabbit's tail to pollinate the plant

Punica granatum

The Punica, better known as the Pomegranate, is grown indoors or in the conservatory mainly for its beautiful bright scarlet flowers, which appear from late spring until well into the summer. The orange-yellow fruit which most people associate with the plant will sometimes be formed on a conservatory-grown specimen, but may well not ripen enough to be edible. Pomegranates require plenty of light during the growing period and pot-grown specimens can be put outside in summer. Pruning is not normally needed for this plant, but straggling or crowded branches can be cut back in early winter if desired.

COMMON NAME
Pomegranate

Stand the pot on a layer of stones to aid drainage

Plant type	Flowering and fruiting shrub
Season of interest	Late spring to autumn
Size	To 180cm (72in); dwarf form to 90cm (36in)
Flower	Single or double, bright orange-red, bell-shaped, 4cm (1½in) across; followed by hard, round, yellow to orange-red fruits
Leaf	Oval, glossy, 2.5cm (1in) long, mid-green
Temperature	13–20°C (55–65°F); rest in winter at minimum 7°C (45F)
Aspect/Light	Brightly-lit situation with plenty of sun during summer
Humidity	Moderate
Watering	Keep compost evenly moist from spring to autumn; keep on the dry side in winter
Feeding	Once every two weeks with liquid fertilizer during spring and summer growing period
Propagation	Plant 7.5 cm (3in) stem cuttings in seed and cutting compost at 16–18°C (61–64°F) in summer
Potting	Potting compost
Problems	Red spider mite, whitefly
Availability	Limited throughout the year
Uses	Grow on its own in large container

Solanum melongena

The Aubergine is easy to grow in the conservatory, and with its purple, edible fruit and large handsome leaves it is both useful and ornamental. The plant is a perennial but it is usually cultivated as an annual. It is suitable for growing in a tub or pot, and will reach up to 90cm (36in) in height. As the fruits form, the plant will need a stake or a wire to support their weight. The variety most often grown is *S. m. esculentum*. This has varying forms, ranging from dark purple fruit, through pale violet to striped purple and white, and pure white. The shape of the fruit may be short and round as well as long and thin.

COMMON NAMES
Aubergine, Egg Plant

Plant type	Flowering and fruiting plant with erect habit
Season of interest	Spring to autumn
Size	To 90cm (36in) when grown in a pot, if not double
Flower	Single, 4cm (1½in) across, purple
Leaf	Irregular oval, 10–20cm (4–8in) long, light green
Temperature	Minimum 5–10°C (40–50°F)
Aspect/Light	Well-lit situation with some direct sunlight
Humidity	Moderate
Watering	Evenly moisten compost throughout growing period, allowing to dry out a little before re-watering
Propagation	Seed grown in early to mid spring in peat-based seed and cutting compost at 18–20°C (65–68°F)
Potting	Peat-based houseplant potting compost
Problems	Whitefly
Availability	Commonly available as seed from early winter; plants from mid to late spring
Uses	Grow on its own in container or conservatory bed

Tie the plant to a wire stretched to the roof for support

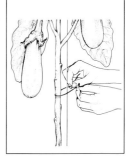

Sparmannia africana

This evergreen flowering shrub from South Africa is a very handsome plant for the conservatory. It has large, heart-shaped, pale green leaves, which are slightly hairy in texture, and clusters of white flowers on long stalks. The flowers are four-petalled, with a prominent tuft of yellow stamens in the centre. Sparmannias can be grown either in the conservatory border or in a large container such as a tub. They need plenty of light but should be protected from direct sun, which can scorch the leaves. These plants grow fast given the right conditions, and if they become too large they can be pruned back hard after the main flush of flowering is over. *S. a.* 'Nana' is a dwarf form, which is suitable as a houseplant.

COMMON NAME
African Hemp

Stand tall, bushy plants in a corner, where they will take up less space

Plant type	Flowering shrub with upright habit
Season of interest	All year round
Size	120–180cm (48–72in)
Flower	Four-petalled, 2.5–5cm (1–2in), white with prominent yellow stamens
Leaf	Heart-shaped, 22.5cm (9in) long, pale green, slightly hairy
Temperature	7–18°C (45–65°F)
Aspect/Light	Well-lit situation with protection from direct sunlight
Humidity	Moderate
Watering	Keep compost evenly moist from spring to autumn; keep on dry side in winter
Feeding	Once every two weeks with liquid fertilizer from early spring to mid summer
Propagation	Plant 10–12.5cm (4–5in) stem cuttings in seed and cutting compost at 18–21°C (65–70°F) in spring
Potting	Houseplant potting compost
Problems	Whitefly, red spider mite
Availability	Limited availability throughout the year
Uses	Grow on its own in large container or conservatory bed

Strelitzia reginae

A spectacular plant with long, paddle-shaped leaves, and orange and blue flowers that arise in a crest from a beak-shaped bud. Some patience is required, as the flowers do not appear until the plant is six or seven years old. The blooms are produced in succession for several weeks from spring to early summer. The Strelitzia needs plenty of space. The leaves can grow up to 125cm (48in) high, and if brushed against they can very easily become ragged. Badly damaged leaves should be removed at the base of the leaf stalk with a sharp knife. When the leaves become dusty or dirty, simply wipe them gently with a damp sponge. The Strelitzia is quite an easy subject to grow, and makes a superb feature plant.

COMMON NAME
Bird of Paradise Flower

Plant type	Flowering plant with erect habit
Season of interest	Spring to early summer
Size	60–125cm (24–49in)
Flower	Unusual, 10–15cm (4–6in), orange and blue, growing from 12.5–20cm (5–8in) horizontal bract
Leaf	Oval, lance-shaped, leathery mid green leaves 20–40cm (8–16in), on 30–60cm (12–24in) stems
Temperature	12–22°C (55–72°F)
Aspect/Light	Well-lit situation with some exposure to sunlight
Humidity	Moderate
Watering	Evenly moisten compost in spring and summer, allowing to dry a little before re-watering; keep on drier side in autumn and winter
Feeding	Once every two to three weeks with flowering plant fertilizer in spring and summer
Propagation	Sow seeds in seed and cutting compost at 24°C (75°F) in spring; divide plant and pot in houseplant potting compost at same temperature in mid to late spring
Potting	Houseplant potting compost
Problems	Scale insect
Availability	Rarely available
Uses	Grow on its own in large container or conservatory bed

After flowering cut off the flower spike with a sharp knife

The Streptocarpus produces its attractive, trumpet-shaped flowers from spring right through until autumn. A variety of bold colours are available, and a beautiful display can be created by massing several different hybrids in a shallow bowl. Faded flowers should be removed with a sharp knife. An interesting propagation technique is to cut a leaf in half down the central vein and gently dib each half into the compost with the cut side down. When the plantlets appear they can be cut apart and potted individually.

COMMON NAMES
Cape Primrose, Cape Cowslip

The plant can be propagated from half a leaf

Plant type	Flowering plant with low-growing habit
Season of interest	Late spring to early autumn
Size	15–30cm (6–12in)
Flower	Five-lobed, tubular, 2.5–5cm (1–2in) across, white, pink, red, blue or mauve, with veined throat, on 10–30cm (4–12in) stalks
Leaf	Strap-shaped, 15–30cm (6–12in), mid to dark green
Temperature	15–22°C (59–72°F)
Aspect/Light	Reasonably well-lit situation, lightly shaded from direct sunlight
Humidity	Moderate to high
Watering	Evenly moisten compost in spring and summer, allowing to dry a little before re-watering; keep on drier side in autumn and winter
Feeding	Half strength flowering plant fertilizer every two to three weeks in spring and summer
Propagation	Sow seeds in seed and cutting compost at 21°C (70°F) in early to mid spring; dib sections of leaf into, or lay entire leaves on, same compost at 20–21°C (68–70°F) in spring
Potting	Houseplant potting compost
Problems	Mealy bug, mildew
Availability	Usually available in spring and summer
Uses	Grow in pot either on its own or as part of group display

Thunbergia alata hybrids

A climbing plant that produces orange to yellow flowers with a dark centre or 'eye', hence the common name of Black-eyed Susan. Given the correct care, the Thunbergia will remain in flower from the end of spring to the beginning of autumn. Dead or dying flowers should be removed before rotting occurs or seeds are set, as either will reduce the flowering period. The plant's twining stems grow vigorously and can completely cover a screen or trellis in the first season. This vigour makes it a particularly useful variety for covering a conservatory wall. Although the Thunbergia is a perennial, the growth can become very leggy and straggly, and the plant is often discarded after the first flowering.

COMMON NAME
Black-eyed Susan

Plant type	Flowering plant with climbing habit
Season of interest	Late spring to early autumn
Size	30–60cm (12–24in)
Flower	Five-lobed, 2.5–5cm (1–2in) across, yellow to orange with dark brown to black centre, growing from tubular base
Leaf	Angular, roughly heart-shaped, crinkly, 5–7.5cm (2–3in), mid green
Temperature	13–19°C (55–66°F)
Aspect/Light	Well-lit situation with exposure to sunlight
Humidity	Moderate
Watering	Evenly moisten compost at beginning of season in spring, adding more water as plant requires
Feeding	Once every two to three weeks with flowering plant fertilizer in spring and summer
Propagation	Sow seeds in seed and cutting compost at 18–19°C (64–66°F) in early spring
Potting	Houseplant potting compost
Problems	Aphid
Availability	Occasionally available from late spring to early summer
Uses	Grow in large container or bed and train up screen, trellis or wall; best used in cooler conservatory

Remove dead flowers to prolong flowering

Trachelospermum jasminoides

An attractive evergreen climber from China, the Trachelospermum has clusters of fragrant white flowers in mid-summer, and grey-green oval leaves. There is also a variegated form, *T. j.* 'Variegatum', whose white-edged leaves take on pink autumn tints which last until the following spring. This plant is suitable for training against a wall or trellis, where it will need to be tied to wires or anchor points. It dislikes very dry conditions and needs plenty of light. Though sometimes slow to become established, the Trachelospermum will reach about 4.6 x 4.6m (15 x 15ft) at maturity.

COMMON NAME
Trachelospermum

Plant type	Flowering plant with climbing habit
Season of interest	Flowers in summer; foliage all year, especially variegated form
Size	To 240cm x 240cm (96 x 96in) if grown in a pot, if not double
Flower	Five-petalled, fragrant, 2.5cm (1in) across, white, in clusters
Leaf	Oval, pointed, up to 11cm (4¼in) long, grey-green or variegated green and white with pink tint in winter
Temperature	Minimum −8°C (17°F) in winter
Aspect/Light	Well-lit situation with some sunlight
Humidity	Moderate
Watering	Keep compost evenly moist from spring to autumn; keep on drier side in winter but do not allow to dry out completely
Feeding	Liquid houseplant fertilizer every month in summer
Propagation	Plant 7.5–10cm (3–4in) stem cuttings in seed and cutting compost at 18–20°C (65–68°F) in summer
Potting	Soil-based potting compost
Problems	Can be slow to establish but worth the wait
Availability	Quite commonly available throughout the year
Uses	Grow in large container or conservatory bed and train up wall or pillar

Grow the plant up a pillar or pole to show off the flowers to best effect

Verbena × hybrida

This colourful perennial may be overwintered in the conservatory, where it makes an ideal container plant. The jewel-like flowers, in shades of bright red, pink, purple and white, form dense, rounded clusters against the attractive grey-green foliage. With adequate water and food, the flowers will be freely produced from early summer to mid-autumn. Regular dead-heading will also encourage repeat flowering. The prostrate varieties are good for displaying in hanging pots or baskets. Established plants can be used for the propagation of new stock for the following season.

COMMON NAME
Verbena

Plant type	Flowering plant with erect or prostrate habit
Season of interest	Early summer to autumn
Size	20–35cm (8–14in)
Flower	Saucer-shaped, in upward-facing clusters, 4–5cm (1½–2cm) across, pink, red, purple, white
Leaf	Oval, 5–8cm (2–3in) long, indented edges, hairy, light grey-green
Temperature	Minimum 5–10°C (40–50°F)
Aspect/Light	Full sun to light shade
Humidity	Moderate
Watering	Evenly moisten compost from spring to autumn, allowing to dry out a little before re-watering; keep on drier side in winter
Feeding	Once every two weeks with flowering plant fertilizer from late spring to early summer
Propagation	Plant stem cuttings in seed and cutting compost at 18–20°C (65–68°F) from late summer to early autumn; sow seed in seed and cutting compost at 13–18°C (55–65°F) in spring
Potting	Houseplant potting compost
Problems	Whitefly
Availability	Commonly available from mid spring to mid summer
Uses	Grow in container or hanging basket

Stand plants with a semi-weeping habit on bricks to enhance the display

Vitis vinifera

Grape Vines have large, lobed leaves, which turn gold or red in autumn, and attractively gnarled stems, but the main attraction is the purple or green, edible fruit. Conservatory-grown vines should be planted in an outside border and trained through into the conservatory to give the roots the space they need. Young plants should be cut back to within (30cm) 12in of soil in early spring and the shoots that follow trained on wires. In the second year after planting, reduce vertical shoots to within 30cm (12in) of origin and reduce side shoots to one bud. Tie in the growths and repeat every year until the required height.

COMMON NAME
Grape Vine

Prune the stems back in early spring

Plant type	Fruiting plant with climbing habit
Season of interest	Late summer to autumn
Size	To 7m (20ft)
Flower	Greenish-yellow, insignificant, followed by round, purple or green, edible fruit in hanging bunches
Leaf	Palmate, 3 or 5 lobed, up to 15cm (6in) long, mid-green, edible when young
Temperature	Minimum 13°C (55°F) in summer and autumn when fruit is ripening
Aspect/Light	Well-lit situation with some direct sunlight
Humidity	Moderate
Watering	As required
Feeding	Houseplant fertilizer in mid spring
Propagation	Plant vine eyes (buds) with a small area of stem, or 10–15cm (4–6in) stem cuttings in winter
Potting	Well-prepared garden soil
Problems	Mildew
Availability	Commonly available throughout the year
Uses	Plant in bed outside conservatory and train through to grow on wall and under roof; best in large conservatory

Eucomis bicolor

A suitable plant for the conservatory, the Pineapple Lily has a thick spike of star-shaped flowers topped by a bushy tuft of leafy bracts which looks very much like the tuft on the top of a pineapple. The flowers themselves are bronze coloured with brown tip markings and are sweetly scented. This plant needs plenty of room as the flower spike grows from a rosette of leaves which can be up to 90cm (36in) in diameter; the flower spike itself is up to 30cm (12in) long. The flowers appear in late summer. After flowering the leaves die back and the plant should be allowed to dry out until growth starts again in spring.

COMMON NAME
Pineapple Lily

Plant type	Flowering bulb with erect habit
Season of interest	Late summer
Size	Height 60cm (24in); spread 90cm (36in)
Flower	Small star-shaped flowers in dense spike up to 30cm (12in) long, bronze coloured with brown tip marking, scented
Leaf	Lance-shaped, to 45cm (18in) long, dark green
Temperature	5–10°C (40–50°F)
Aspect/Light	Well-lit situation
Watering	Water regularly during growing season; allow to dry out as leaves wither in late summer
Feeding	Once every two to three weeks with flowering plant fertilizer during spring and early summer
Propagation	Divide bulbous clumps in autumn; sow seeds in seed and cutting compost at 16°C (61°F) in spring
Potting	Houseplant potting compost
Problems	None
Availability	Commonly available as dormant bulbs in early spring
Uses	Grow in container either on its own or as part of group display
Other varieties	*E. comosa* – pale yellow flowers

Group the Eucomis with plants of different heights and shapes

Sweet-smelling, colourful Freesias carry their tubular flowers on strong arching stems. Always popular as cut flowèrs, they will also provide a good display in the conservatory, where the bulbs can be grown in pots or wooden boxes with relative ease. The flowering period lasts from late winter to mid spring, and there are many different named cultivars in a wide range of colours from white and pale yellow, through orange, pink and red to mauve and blue. Freesias can be grown either from corms or from seed. When flowering has finished, continue to feed and water the plants well until the leaves start to die down. Then allow them to dry out and store in a well-aired place until the start of the next growing season.

COMMON NAME
Freesia

The Freesia is a good plant to grow in a wooden box filled with potting compost

Plant type	Flowering bulb with arching habit
Season of interest	Late winter to mid-spring
Size	30–45cm (12–18in)
Flower	Tubular, 2.5–5cm (1–2in), white, yellow, orange, pink, red, mauve or blue
Leaf	Long, narrow, 22.5cm (9in), dark green
Temperature	Minimum 10–15°C (50–60°F)
Aspect/Light	Well-lit situation with sunlight
Humidity	Moderate
Watering	Keep compost evenly moist during growing period; allow to dry out once flowering is over and leaves begin to wither
Feeding	Once every two weeks with flowering plant fertilizer from appearance of flower buds until flowering is over
Propagation	Separate corm offsets in late summer; sow seeds in seed sowing compost at 15–21°C (60–70°F) in early spring
Potting	Soil-based potting compost
Problems	None
Availability	Corms widely available from late summer to autumn; seed from early to mid spring
Uses	Grow in container for seasonal interest

Galtonia candicans

Also known as the Summer Hyacinth, and closely related to the true Hyacinth, this is a very attractive late summer-flowering bulb for the cool conservatory. The Galtonia has hanging, bell-shaped, scented white flowers on tall spikes, which are up to 90cm (36in) high. The upright flower stems grow from a rosette of strap-shaped, light-green leaves. The large, round bulbs are suitable for growing in a pot or tub. They should be planted in groups of three or five, for a good display, with the necks of the bulbs pushed just below the soil surface. After flowering has finished, the bulbs can be planted out separately, or lifted and stored dry for replanting in spring.

COMMON NAME
Summer Hyacinth

Plant type	Flowering bulb with upright habit
Season of interest	Late summer to early autumn
Size	60–90cm (24–36in)
Flower	Bell-shaped, 4cm (1½in) long, carried in groups of 12 or more along upright stems, scented, white shaded green
Leaf	Strap-shaped, 30–45cm (12–18in) long, upright, eventually spreading, light green to grey-green
Temperature	Minimum 5–10°C (40–50°F) in growing season
Aspect/Light	Full sun to light shade
Humidity	Moderate
Watering	Keep compost evenly moist while plant is in growth; keep dormant bulb dry
Feeding	Feed with liquid fertilizer as flowers fade
Propagation	Remove and replant bulblets every 5 years
Potting	Bulb fibre or houseplant potting compost
Problems	Slugs and snails can damage leaves and flowers
Availability	As dormant bulbs from late winter to early spring; as plants from mid to late summer
Uses	Grow in container for seasonal colour

Support the stems using green split canes and wire rings

Lilium hybrids

Lilies are perhaps the most spectacular of the summer-flowering bulbs, with large, scented flowers in a wide variety of colours. Many Lilium species grow well in containers and are ideal for the conservatory or as indoor plants as pots of forced bulbs can be purchased to flower at any time of year. Home-planted lilies need a good potting medium and adequate watering and feeding. Bulbs should be kept cold, dark and damp until they shoot, then moved into the light. It is best to plant out old bulbs in the garden and purchase new bulbs for pots. There are many varieties suitable for container growing.

COMMON NAME
Lily

To propagate the Lily, remove the bubules and pot them up separately

Plant type	Flowering bulb with upright habit
Season of interest	Summer
Size	6–15m (24–60in)
Flower	Trumpet-, funnel- or turban-shaped, 10–25cm (4–10in) long, white, yellow, gold, orange, red
Leaf	Lance-shaped, 7.5–15cm (3–6in) long, glossy, mid to dark green
Temperature	Night-time temperature should remain under 10°C (50°F) during growing season
Aspect/Light	Well-lit situation out of direct sun
Humidity	Moderate
Watering	Keep compost evenly moist at all times during growing season; allow to dry out once flowering has finished and leaves start to yellow
Feeding	Houseplant liquid fertilizer as flowers are dying to build up bulbs for next season
Propagation	Remove and replant side bulblets
Potting	Houseplant potting compost
Problems	Slugs and vine weevils may damage bulbs; grow in pots for only one year
Availability	Commonly available autumn and early winter; late winter and early spring as dormant bulbs
Uses	Grow in container for seasonal interest; prefers cooler conservatory

Nerine bowdenii

The bright pink flowers of this handsome South African bulb provide a welcome splash of colour in the conservatory. The flower heads have an elegant and highly distinctive shape, being composed of clusters of trumpet-shaped flowers and tall, straight stems. A good cultivar to grow is *N. b.* 'Pink Trumpet', a late-flowering variety that has silver-pink flowers with a more open shape. Nerines prefer a cool conservatory, where they grow well in large containers. If possible, these plants should not be moved at all after they have flowered as any disturbance to their roots is likely to prevent them from flowering during the following season.

COMMON NAME
Nerine

Plant type	Flowering bulb with erect habit
Season of interest	Late summer to autumn
Size	45–60cm (18–24in)
Flower	Narrow-petalled trumpets, 10–12.5cm (4–5in) wide, borne in clusters with or after foliage
Leaf	Strap-shaped, 45–53cm (18–21in) long, mid to dark-green
Temperature	0–3°C (32–37°)
Aspect/Light	Full sun
Humidity	Moderate
Watering	Keep compost evenly moist from spring to autumn; keep drier after flowering until new growth appears
Feeding	Once every two to three weeks with flowering plant liquid fertilizer once new leaves appear and continue until mid winter
Propagation	Plant dormant bulbs in mid to late summer; divide existing clumps in mid summer prior to flowering
Potting	Soil-based compost with 25 per cent extra grit or sharp sand
Problems	Root disturbance can prevent flowering the following year
Availability	Quite commonly available as dormant bulbs from late summer to early autumn or as pot plants in leaf in early spring
Uses	Grow in large container either on its own or grouped with other flowering plants

Lay pots on their side from spring to early summer to 'rest' the bulb

Many tulips make excellent pot plants for the conservatory or indoors, where they can flower from as early as Christmas through to mid-late spring. A cool conservatory is ideal. Most tulips are suitable for container planting, from the early-flowering hybrids and species tulips to the taller Darwin and Lily-flowered varieties. They can be grown in bulb fibre and houseplant potting compost, or, if they are to be planted out after flowering, in seed and cutting compost. In this case they will need to be fed with flowering plant fertilizer from the time the flower buds appear to feed the bulbs for the next season.

COMMON NAME
Tulip

Pot bulbs in a bowl containing compost over a layer of bulb fibre

Plant type	Flowering bulb with erect habit
Season of interest	Winter to late spring
Size	12.5–75cm (5–30in)
Flower	6-pointed, oval or fringed petals, 4–8cm (1½–3in) wide and deep, white, cream, yellow, orange, pink, red, mauve, often variegated
Leaf	Lance-shaped, 15–23cm (6–9in) long, tapering, olive-green
Temperature	4–7°C (40–45°F)
Aspect/Light	Full sun to light shade
Humidity	Moderate
Watering	Evenly moisten compost throughout growing period, allowing to dry out a little before re-watering
Feeding	Once every two weeks after flower buds appear
Propagation	Plant dry bulbs from September to October
Potting	Bulb fibre and houseplant potting compost
Problems	None
Availability	Commonly available as dormant bulbs from late summer to early winter and in pots from mid winter to mid spring
Uses	Grow on its own in container for seasonal interest

Aloe variegata

A highly distinctive succulent with a rosette of very thick, triangular leaves coloured dark green with whitish bands and edges. In spring the plant produces a long flower spike bearing a number of tubular flowers. The Aloe can tolerate a wide range of conditions and a certain amount of neglect. It is at its most attractive when young and compact. After a while the stem tends to become rather untidy and the plant can become top-heavy, losing its original elegant, symmetrical shape as it leans to one side. Although a clay pot will help to provide stability, the appearance of the plant may eventually become so lop-sided as to warrant being replaced with a younger specimen. New plants can be propagated fairly easily from offsets that grow in the soil.

COMMON NAME
Partridge-breasted Aloe

Plant type	Flowering succulent with erect habit
Season of interest	Spring to early summer
Size	15–80cm (6–32in)
Flower	Tubular, 2.5cm (1in), pink, on 10–20cm (4–8in) stem, produced from early spring to summer
Leaf	Pointed, 7.5–12.5cm (3–5in) long, 2.5–4cm (1–1½in) wide, thick, fleshy, dark green with whitish bands and edges, borne in rosette on stem
Temperature	10–28°C (50–82°F)
Aspect/Light	Well-lit situation with some sunlight
Humidity	Low
Watering	Evenly moisten compost in spring and summer, allowing to dry a little before re-watering; water just enough to prevent dehydration in autumn and winter
Feeding	Once every three to four weeks with flowering plant fertilizer in spring and summer
Propagation	Remove offsets and plant in cactus and succulent compost at 18–20°C (65–68°F) in late spring to early summer
Potting	Cactus and succulent compost
Problems	Mealy bug, root mealy bug, rot from too much water
Availability	Commonly available throughout year
Uses	Grow on its own in container
Other varieties	A. aristata – more compact rosette; orange flowers

Remove damaged or withered leaves with a sharp knife

Epiphyllum × 'Ackermannii'

Few plants can produce anything to match the large and extraordinarily beautiful flowers of the Epiphyllum. The flowers appear along the edges of the curious, flat or angular stems, which are initially erect, but lay outwards as they grow. It may become necessary to support the stems with a stake. Take care when performing this task or otherwise tending to the plant as the stems bear spines. Unlike most other cacti, this cactus is an epiphytic or tree-living plant. Not only does it prefer compost with a higher humus content, but it also dislikes direct sunlight, requiring a position with light shade.

COMMON NAME
Orchid Cactus

Provide support for wayward stems

Plant type	Flowering cactus with erect habit
Season of interest	Spring, occasionally summer
Size	30–45cm (4–6in)
Flower	10–15cm (4–6in), red, with radiating petals with protruding stamens, produced in spring/summer
Leaf	Erect, angular, flattish, green stems, 30–45cm (12–18in) long, 2.5–5cm (1–2in) wide
Temperature	10–24°C (50–75°F)
Aspect/Light	Moderate light with some light shade
Humidity	Moderate to high
Watering	Evenly moisten compost in spring and summer; keep on dry side in autumn and winter, watering only enough to prevent dehydration
Feeding	Once every two to three weeks with flowering plant fertilizer from early spring until flowers are well formed
Propagation	10–15cm (4–6in) cuttings or side shoots in cactus and succulent compost at 20–22°C (68–72°F) in mid spring to early summer, sow seeds at 24–27°C (75–80°F)
Potting	Cactus and succulent compost or houseplant potting compost
Problems	Mealy bug
Availability	Occasionally available in spring
Uses	Grow on its own in container
Other varieties	E. × 'Cooperi' – fragrant, white flowers

Gymnocalycium andreae

The diminutive Gymnocalycium is a small plant that makes a worthwhile contribution to a collection of cacti and succulents grown either on a sunny windowsill or in a conservatory. It is attractive throughout the year, but at its best when it comes into bloom, producing yellow flowers that are so large they almost dwarf the plant. The chin-shaped nodules, or tubercles, on the plant have earned it the common name of Chin Cactus. As with propagating other cacti, it is wise to allow the cut edges of the offsets to dry out a little for a day or so before inserting them into the compost. Take care when choosing the varieties of the plant, as some produce quite fierce spines for their size.

COMMON NAME
Chin Cactus

Plant type	Flowering cactus with low-growing, globular habit
Season of interest	Summer
Size	5cm (2in)
Flower	Radiating petals forming yellow flowers, 2.5cm (1in) wide
Leaf	Globular, greyish green stem with small spines
Temperature	7–30°C (45–86°F)
Aspect/Light	Direct sun
Humidity	Low
Watering	Evenly moisten compost in spring and summer, allowing to dry out a little before re-watering; keep on the dry side in autumn and winter, watering just enough to prevent dehydration
Feeding	Once every two to three weeks with half strength flowering plant fertilizer in spring and summer
Propagation	Plant offsets in cactus and succulent compost at 21–22°C (70–72°F) in late spring to early summer
Potting	Cactus and succulent compost
Problems	Mealy bug
Availability	Occasionally available in spring and summer
Uses	Grow on its own in container
Other varieties	G. baldianum – pink or red flowers
G. denudatum – white flowers

Leave offsets for a couple of days to allow the cut surfaces to dry and heal

If cared for correctly, the Lobivia will reward the owner with a spectacular display of colourful flowers, quite out of proportion to the diminutive plant that bears them. Although the individual flowers do not last very long, they are produced in succession and the display may last for several weeks. The appeal of the plant is further enhanced by the fact that the flowers open in the morning and close in the evening. Particular care should be taken with watering, as too much water can quite easily cause root rot followed by the loss of the plant. This is especially important during the winter when the plant is dormant.

COMMON NAME
Cob Cactus

Plant type	Flowering cactus with globular habit
Season of interest	Late spring and summer
Size	7.5–10cm (3–4in)
Flower	Rayed petals forming red flowers, 2.5–5cm (1–2in), produced late spring/summer
Leaf	Globular, ribbed, green stem becoming more cylindrical with age
Temperature	10–28°C (50–82°F)
Aspect/Light	Well-lit situation in full sun
Humidity	Low
Watering	Evenly moisten compost in spring and summer, allowing to dry a little before re-watering; provide only sufficient to prevent dehydration in autumn and winter
Feeding	Once every two to three weeks with half strength flowering plant fertilizer in spring and summer
Propagation	Carefully tease apart offsets and pot in cactus and succulent compost at 20–22°C (68–72°F) in spring and summer
Potting	Cactus and succulent compost
Problems	Mealy bug, root mealy bug, root rot from over-watering
Availability	Occasionally available spring and early summer
Uses	Grow on its own in container
Other varieties	L. hertrichiana – slightly larger; red flowers

Gently tease offsets apart, wearing gloves for protection

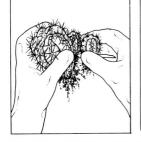

Opuntia microdasys albispina

The Opuntia is a popular cactus, with an unusual, unpredictable habit of growth. The leaf pads are produced in an irregular pattern so that each plant looks different. The tissue on the pads is dotted with areoles from which hooked bristles called glochids emerge. The glochids look attractive, but can be a nuisance as even the most casual contact will dislodge them from the plant. Once in the skin they are very difficult to remove and produce a pain or irritation not dissimilar to that caused by fibres of fibreglass. With all Opuntia avoid leaving water droplets on the plant, as marking or scorching can easily occur in sunlight. Opuntia are good plants to use in cactus gardens.

COMMON NAMES
Prickly Pear, Bunny Ears

Plant type	Ornamental cactus with upright habit
Season of interest	All year round
Size	10–30cm (4–12in)
Flower	4cm (1½in) wide, yellow, rarely produced, in summer
Leaf	Oval leaf pads, 5–7.5cm (2–3in), green with reddish brown glochids
Temperature	10–28°C (50–82°F)
Aspect/Light	Full sun
Humidity	Low
Watering	Evenly moisten compost in spring and summer, allowing to dry a little before re-watering; water only enough to prevent dehydration in autumn and winter
Feeding	Once every two to three weeks with half strength flowering plant fertilizer in spring and summer
Propagation	Remove pad in spring or summer; allow wound to dry for a few days to produce a callus, then pot in cactus and succulent compost at 20–22°C (68–72°F); sow seeds as above in spring
Potting	Cactus and succulent compost
Problems	Mealy bug, root mealy bug
Availability	Occasionally available throughout year
Uses	Grow in container either on its own or as part of cactus collection
Other varieties	O. m. rufida – reddish brown glochids O. robusta – larger; pronounced spines

Glochids can be removed from the skin with adhesive tape

Rebutia senilis 'Elegans'

For its size the Rebutia is a prolifically flowering plant, becoming virtually smothered in fiery-red blossoms for several days. The small plants produce clumps of offsets, as well as seedling plants, which occasionally grow to 15–20cm (6–8in) wide. The effect, when in flower, is quite spectacular. Offsets develop the colour of the parent plant and can complement the display as the population grows, whereas seedlings often produce a range of colours due to their mixed parentage, including white, yellow, orange and red. As well as being suitable for display on its own, the Rebutia can be used effectively in bowl arrangements.

Gently tease offsets apart, wearing gloves for protection

Plant type	Flowering cactus with globular habit
Season of interest	Late spring, early summer
Size	5cm (2in)
Flower	2.5–4cm (1–1½in), fiery-red flowers, produced in late spring/early summer
Leaf	Small, globular green stem with soft white spines
Temperature	10–28°C (50–82°F)
Aspect/Light	Full sun
Humidity	Low
Watering	Evenly moisten compost in spring and summer, allowing to dry a little before re-watering; keep on the dry side in autumn and winter, watering only enough to prevent dehydration
Feeding	Once every two to three weeks with flowering plant fertilizer in spring and summer
Propagation	Remove offsets in late spring to early summer and plant in cactus and succulent compost at 20–22°C (68–72°F); sow seeds in spring
Potting	Cactus and succulent compost
Problems	Mealy bug, root mealy bug
Availability	Quite commonly available in spring and summer
Uses	Grow in container either on its own or as part of cactus display
Other varieties	*R. fiebrigii* – orange flowers

Stapelia variegata

The Stapelia is an unusual plant with fleshy, angular stems that spread across the pot. The flowers, produced from summer to autumn, are also unusual, being quite fleshy, arranged in a star-like pattern, and borne at a strange angle at the side of the plant. In proportion to the plant they are also quite large. However, the most unusual characteristic of the plant is the smell of the flowers, which is quite revolting and resembles the smell of carrion, hence the common name of Carrion Flower. This smell has the purpose of attracting flies, which would normally feast on rotting meat, to pollinate the flowers. The odour can be so strong that it fills a room, in which case the flower is perhaps best removed.

COMMON NAMES
Carrion Flower, Star Flower, Toad Plant

Plant type	Flowering succulent with low-growing, erect, spreading habit
Season of interest	Summer, autumn
Size	7.5–15cm (3–6in)
Flower	Star-like, five-lobed, 6.5cm (2½in), yellow with reddish brown flecks and lines, with revolting smell of carrion, produced summer/autumn
Leaf	Angular, branching stems, 7.5–15cm (3–6in), fleshy, grey-green
Temperature	10–28°C (50–82°F)
Aspect/Light	Full sun
Humidity	Low
Watering	Barely moisten compost in spring and summer, allowing to almost dry out before re-watering; keep on the dry side in autumn and winter
Feeding	Once a month with half strength flowering plant fertilizer in spring and summer
Propagation	Sow seeds in cactus and succulent compost at 20–22°C (68–72°F) in mid spring; divide or cut 10cm (4in) stem and plant as above from late spring to mid summer
Potting	Cactus and succulent compost
Problems	Mealy bug, root mealy bug, root rot
Availability	Occasionally available spring and summer
Uses	Grow on its own in container
Other varieties	*S. hirsuta* – purplish brown flower

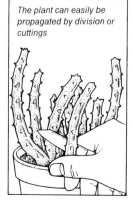

The plant can easily be propagated by division or cuttings

Billbergia nutans

A very hardy plant, the Billbergia can tolerate lower temperatures than many other bromeliads, down to 10°C (50°F). It does not have a specific flowering season, and can bloom at almost any time of year, producing attractive, pendulous flowers from its pink-bracted flower stems. Offsets are formed prolifically and if not removed the display can look untidy. Leaf tips that wither due to

dehydration can be trimmed off, taking care to leave a small edge of dead tissue. However, it is obviously better to

avoid the need for this by maintaining the level of humidity.
COMMON NAME
Queen's Tears

Trim untidy leaf ends with a sharp pair of scissors

Plant type	Flowering bromeliad with upright habit
Season of interest	Varies according to plant and situation
Size	30–45cm (12–18in)
Flower	Small, pink and blue, hanging from 5–7.5cm (2–3in) long, pink bracts, borne on 30cm (12in) spikes, produced at any time of year
Leaf	Strap-like, thin, 30–45cm (12–18in) long
Temperature	10–20°C (50–68°F)
Aspect/Light	Well-lit position with some direct sunlight
Humidity	Moderate to high
Watering	Evenly moisten compost throughout year, allowing to dry a little before re-watering
Feeding	Once every two to three weeks with houseplant fertilizer in spring and summer
Propagation	Remove 10–15cm (4–6in) offsets in spring and pot in houseplant potting or bromeliad compost at 18–20°C (64–68°F)
Potting	Houseplant potting or bromeliad compost
Problems	Mealy bug, dehydration of leaf ends in dry atmosphere
Availability	Occasionally available from spring to summer
Uses	Grow on its own in container

Fascicularia bicolor

This native of Chile is one of the finest bromeliads. Although it comes from a warm climate, its herbaceous, perennial habit, and close, spiny, leathery rosettes of leaves help it to tolerate a wide range of conditions. It has pale blue flowers surrounded by ivory-coloured bracts with serrated edges. Given a peaty soil with sand added to improve drainage, it can be successfully cultivated in many locations. It can even be grown without a pot, simply by putting a layer of moss with a mixture of peat and sand over some rocks. The Fascicularia is an ideal plant for the cooler conservatory, provided the temperature is kept over 3°C (37°F).

Plant type	Flowering bromeliad with horizontal, radiating habit
Season of interest	All year round
Size	50–60cm (18–24in)
Flower	Up to 3.5cm (1¼in) long, surrounded by ivory-coloured bracts, up to 4cm (1½) long, serrated
Leaf	Lance-shaped, 50cm (18in) or more long, green
Temperature	3–28°C (37–82°F)
Aspect/Light	Light shade
Humidity	Moderate
Watering	Evenly moisten compost in spring and summer; keep on drier side in autumn and winter; never allow compost to become waterlogged
Feeding	Liquid houseplant fertilizer in late spring
Propagation	Remove offsets in spring or early summer and pot in houseplant potting or bromeliad compost at 27°C (80°F); slow to root
Potting	Houseplant potting or bromeliad compost
Problems	Whitefly, mealy bug
Availability	Quite commonly available in spring and summer
Uses	Grow on its own in container

To propagate the plant, remove the side shoots and pot them up singly

Index

Index

Acknowledgements

The publishers would like to thank the following for supplying photographs for this book.

Page 20 Flower Council of Holland; 21, 22, 23 Paul Forrester; 24 Harry Smith; 25 Brian Davis; 30 Peter Stiles; 35 Garden Picture Library; 37 Garden Picture Library; 39 Harry Smith; 47, 48 Harry Smith; 49, 50 Flower Council of Holland; 51 Harry Smith; 53 Flower Council of Holland; 54 Harry Smith; 58 Flower Council of Holland; 59, 60 Brian Davis; 61 A-Z Botanical Collection; 62, 63 Brian Davis; 64 Harry Smith; 65, 66 Flower Council of Holland; 67, 68 Brian Davis; 70 Brian Davis; 71 Garden Picture Library; 72 Harry Smith; 73 Brian Davis; 74 Harry Smith; 75 Brian Davis; 77 Garden Picture Library; 80 Flower Council of Holland; 81 Brian Davis; 82 Paul Forrester; 83, 84, 85, 86 Brian Davis; 87 Harry Smith; 88 A-Z Botanical Collection; 92 Brian Davis; 93 Harry Smith; 94, 95 Brian Davis; 96 Garden Picture Library; 97 A-Z Botanical Collection; 98 Flower Council of Holland; 100, 101 Harry Smith; 102, 103, 104 Brian Davis; 105 A-Z Botanical Collection; 106, 107 Brian Davis; 108 A-Z Botanical Collection; 109 Brian Davis; 111, 112, 113, 115, 116, 117, 118 Harry Smith.

All other photographs by Paul Forrester.